Lifting the Veil

Lifting the Veil

Jane Kamerling

Fred Gustafson

fisher king press

COPYRIGHT

Published simultaneously in Canada, the United Kingdom, and the United States of America by Fisher King Press. For information on obtaining permission for use of material from this work, submit a written request to:

permissions@fisherkingpress.com

Fisher King Press
PO Box 222321
Carmel, CA 93922
www.fisherkingpress.com
fisherking@fisherkingpress.com
+1-831-238-7799

Many thanks to all who have directly or indirectly provided permission to quote their works. Every effort has been made to trace all copyright holders; however, if any have been overlooked, the authors will be pleased to make the necessary arrangements at the first opportunity.

CONTENTS

ACKNOWLEDGEMENTS

My first thanks goes to my father, William Kamerling, who died at 96 setting an example of a person who through determination accomplishes what's important and has made me believe that no goal is too high or unreachable.

Thanks to Andrew Samuels who was the first person with whom we discussed the book concept. He helped us formulate our ideas and led us to others who have contributed to this area of study. I want to thank Betul Basaran, my teacher at University of Chicago's Continuing Adult Education Program. She presented an understanding of Muslim women from a variety of different viewpoints. She was the person who connected me to the *Flying Broom* in Ankara where I met Halime Guner. Interviewing Halime Guner was the highlight experience of writing this book. I had difficulty contacting her and therefore contacted her at the very last moment. She was out of town and returned the only day that I was *able* to be in Ankara. I believe meeting her was a synchronicity that brought together all the dreams and ideas I had in creating this book. She *is* the embodiment of our heroic Sheherazade, changing the landscape for Muslim Turkish Women and therefore for men and women universally. Halime, I thank you deeply as well as to the other women and men who are raising consciousness, you reinforce my optimism about humanity.

Thanks to my family and friends, especially Norm Futrell, who listened forever about what I was learning. I also give special attention to my children for enriching my life and being a part of my spirit that I bring to all my endeavors. Special thanks to Cathy Jones, Gus Cwik and Nancy Dougherty for giving me ideas and books to read. Thomas Singer and Sam Kimbles gave us the structure to hold our book by writing their book, *Cultural Complex*. Thank you, Tom, for getting excited about our work and encouraging us to continue with it. Rinda West helped us make sense of our writing and gave fluidity to our thoughts.

Jane Kamerling

As my co-author has stated, gratitude goes to many people, places and books that have brought this project to completion. When she approached me a few years ago to co-write with her on this theme of the veil, my first reaction was hardly enthusiastic. However, as she referred readings to me, my interests perked and then carried me into a world of which most of us in the Western world know little. So my thanks go to Jane for her invitation to co-write and her trust in my ability to do so.

I was particularly grateful to have read the complete unabridged work of the *Thousand Nights and One Night*. Here was a mother lode of Eastern fairy tales that seemed to hold a key for what this book partly tries to unlock. In addition, it was a book by Maria Rosa Menocal, *Ornament of the World*, that inspired my wife and I to visit key cities in the Andalusian area of Spain, the once major center of the golden era of Islam. It was here I became deeply aware of what once was and what the heart of Islam may be trying to regain.

Thanks go to the North American Council of Jungian Societies for inviting us to speak at their national gathering in Chicago in 2005 and again to the Inter-Regional Society for Jungian Analysts to present this same material in Santa Fe, New Mexico in 2006. We were well received which encouraged us to proceed. Gratitude goes to our many colleagues at the Chicago Jung Institute, my friends and helpful critics, Robert Henderson, Dudley Tyler, and William Baugh with whom I consulted along the way of this writing and to Vian Abdulrahman, a wonderful Kurdish woman, who in December 1996 along with her people fled the onslaughts of Saddam Hussein. We both are grateful to Rinda West for the excellent and thorough editing she provided and for her encouragement to proceed with this project. Finally, I thank my partner and wife, Karen, of many years, for her loving support and continued encouragement as well as to my two adult children, Andrea and Aaron, who have always been interested in my work, and, in their own unique and gifted way, lifted the veil of my own consciousness regarding the world in which we now live.

Fred Gustafson

FOREWORD

Thomas Singer, M.D.

In her chapter "The Symbol of the Veil," Jane Kamerling writes in this book of her seeing an Arab woman standing alone on top of a hill as night approached in the desert forty-five years ago: "Hidden under the robes that concealed her body was a world unknown to me." This becomes the central, symbolic image of the authors' quest of *Lifting the Veil.* Many meanings of this multivalent and potent symbol emerge in the journey to unveil to Westerners the foreign world of Arab Muslims. There is one potential, perhaps unintended, meaning of "Lifting the Veil" that occurred to me while reading this unique study. Could it be that the title of the book also boomerangs back onto the long veiled Jungian tradition of only looking at the world through our own very particular point of view— which is frequently quite blind and deaf to what is happening around us?

The point that I want to underline in this preface is that our own Jungian veil is being lifted in this book and others like it that are beginning to appear in our literature. This veil is our longstanding attitude toward the outer, collective world. Burned by his disastrous experience of speaking out on the rise of Nazism in the 1930s and his ill timed foray into discussing the still intriguing notion of national character, Jung and his followers for the next fifty years or so remained relatively quiet, perhaps even in retreat from, political, social, and cultural issues in favor of a primary, introverted focus on the individual and the individuation process. Most commentary about more collective matters used the theory of archetypes to explain what was happening in the psyche of the world. Over time, it has become rather tiring to me to see in our tradition how most collective events are reduced to or interpreted as some appearance of the Shadow or the Self or the Hero or the Feminine. The mention of archetypal patterns in collective life has begun to sound to me as if we can't stop building our own theoretical Walmarts on the outskirts of increasingly homogenized urban and rural landscapes. As with globalization itself, the Jungian vocabulary for describing the world has become less and less meaningful as the particularity of place, landscape, history, economics, ethnicity, and every other distinguishing cultural characteristic gets ignored or glossed over in our universalizing, archetypal constructs.

This book reverses that trend by taking into account those levels of the psyche that Jung himself had outlined in a 1926 diagram of the psyche in which he displayed an almost geological/evolutionary vision of the psyche. At the very top of the diagram was the tiny ego, embedded in the family. In successive layers of the psyche as it plunged underwater, Jung indicated ever deepening realms in the following order: clans, nations, large groups (European man for example), primate ancestors, animal ancestors in general, and, at the very bottom of the human psyche lay the "central fire."

The vast middle range of the psyche which included everything between clans and large groups that Jung himself diagrammed in 1926 was mostly ignored by those next generations of Jungians who followed in his footsteps. Their emphasis has been on the individual above and/or the archetypal realm in the lower depths which presumably emanate out of the "central fire." I believe it is fair to say that the Jungians have mostly veiled themselves from taking into full consideration the reality and importance of the social, political, and cultural dimensions of the psyche as it resides in individuals, clans, tribes, nations, and the world.

This book is not only making an effort to unveil the world of Arab Muslims to the Western world, it is participating in the unveiling of Jungians and the Jungian point of view to a much broader way of understanding the psyche of individuals and groups. It takes into account the vicissitudes of place, history, culture, and all those forces that shape the psyche of the collective and the individual.

If Jung was right that the human race hangs by the thin thread of the human psyche, exploring and understanding the cultural or social level of the psyche in all its complexities and differences is an essential undertaking in making that thread a little stronger. Our misadventures in the Middle East bare ample evidence to how costly it can be when we fail to understand how different Americans and other westerners are from much of the world. This book takes a big step in the direction of exploring and understanding these essential levels of the human psyche and I salute Jane Kamerling and Fred Gustafson for their effort at "lifting the veil."

Thomas Singer, M.D. is a Jungian Diplomate Analyst with the C.G. Jung Institute of San Francisco, California. He currently serves as Editor of the Analytical Psychology and Contemporary Culture Series for Spring Journal Books and his new contributions in that series appear in *Psyche and the City: A Soul's Guide to the Modern Metropolis*, *Ancient Greece, Modern Psyche* and *Placing Psyche: Exploring Cultural Complexes in Australia*.

TIMELINE OF HISTORICAL EVENTS

Early Second Millennium B.C.E.	Abraham, the father of the prophetic religions God gives the Ten Commandments on Mt. Sinai.
Essenes	Time of the Dead Sea Scrolls.
1000 B.C.E.	Jews led out of slavery to the Promised Land.
1500 B.C.E.	God gives law on Mt. Sinai.
500 B.C.E.	Writing of the Torah (Old testament).
586 B.C.E.	Promised Land conquered. Regained fifty years later (Greek Influence).
1000 B.C.E.	Conquered Promise Land (King David).
3rd Century B.C.E.	Jewish interpretive process - solidifying bible. Birth of Christ
70 C.E.	Destruction of second temple. Conquered by the Romans.
Late 1st Century	Gospels written by John and Paul.
234-634 C.E.	Sasanian Empire (Iran).
330 C.E.	Center of Catholicism transferred from Constantinople to Rome.
570 C.E.	Birth of Muhammad.
7th Century	Byzantine (Christian) and Persian (Zoroastrianism) Empires dominate the world.
610 C.E.	First revelation from Allah.
622 C.E.	Hijra-migration from Mecca to Medina - beginning of Islamic calendar.
632 C.E.	Muhammad's death. Caliphs (successors): first four called the *Rashidun* (rightly guarded).
632-634 C.E.	Abu Bakr
634-644 C.E.	Umar
644-656 C.E.	Uthman - murdered.
656-661 C.E.	Ali- murdered- prophets cousin, blood - relative beginning of split in Islam *Shi's* and *Sunnis*.
661-680 C.E.	Umayyad dynasty moved *Caliphate* to Damascus - 5th *Caliph*.

680 C.E.	Islam conquered North Africa (Tunasia, Algeria, Morocco to the Atlantic Ocean).
685 C.E.	Islamic borders widen to China.
713-1031 C.E.	Berbers conquered Spain beginning the Andalusian Empire.
750-1258 C.E.	Abbasids defeated Umayyads and re-established *Caliphate* in Baghdad.
846 C.E.	Islam sacked Rome.
8th Century	Islam conquered Spain, Portugal and invaded France.
9th Century	Islam conquered Sicily.
1000 C.E.	Conquered kingdom of Saba (pre-Islamic Yemen).
1096-1099 C.E.	1st Crusade - capture of Jerusalem.
1146-1148 C.E.	2nd Crusade - siege of Damascus fails.
1189-1192 C.E.	3rd Crusade - capture of Acre but fail to recapture Jerusalem.
1201-1204 C.E.	4th Crusade - conquer Constantinople.
1217-1221 C.E.	5th Crusade - attacked Egypt.
1057 C.E.	Fatimids conquer Egypt.
1187 C.E.	Salahadin victorious over Crusaders, Thirteenth Century - Muslims rule Russia, Vienna, Hungary and Eastern Europe.
13th Century	Gangis Khan conquered the Abbasids, expanded to Anatolia and the Mongols ruled until 1380.
15th Century	Russia expels Muslims.
1453 C.E.	End of WW 1 – Ottoman Empire.
1500-1722 C.E.	Safavid Dynasty (Persia).
1526-1738 C.E.	Mughal Dynasty (India).
1948 C.E.	Establishment of the State of Israel.
1979 C.E.	Islamic revolution in Iran.
1992 C.E.	First Iraq War.
2001 C.E.	Attack on the two World Trade Towers in New York (9-11).
2003 C.E.	Second Iraq War.

INTRODUCTION

Not Christian, or Jew or Muslim, Not Hindu, Buddhist, Sufi, or Zen.
Not any religion
Or cultural system. I am not from the east or the west,
Not out of the ocean or up
From the ground, not natural or ethereal, not
Composed of elements at all.
I do not exist.
Am not an entity in this world. Or the next,
Did not descend from Adam and Eve or any
Origin story. My place is the placeless, a trace
Of the traceless.
Neither body nor soul.
I belong to the beloved, have seen the two worlds as one
And that one can call to and know.
First, last, outer, inner,
Only that breath breathing Human Being.

Rumi

The devastation and shock of 9/11 reached every community in America. It raised questions never before considered. Inspired by that event, research became critical to organize our thinking and make sense out of nonsense and organization out of chaos. Political literature addressing the dynamics leading up to the catastrophe of the collapse of the Twin Towers has been prolific as the urgency to understand the Islamic world has increased. International relations theory offers a variety of concepts of why and how nations may respond to one another for expansion, defense, or peace. These theories develop with objective quantifiable equations and leave no

1

room for immeasurable, subjective variables. Perception is one of those variables that cannot be left out of the equation when looking at what motivates nations and international diplomacy. As Jungian analysts, we wanted to contribute to this body of knowledge by analyzing an underlying psychological dynamic that fuels the conflict between the West and the Islamic world. To that end, we have distilled information from a variety of readings, interviews, documentaries and personal experiences in the Islamic world. This book attempts to bring some awareness to the unconscious and underlying dynamics that are reflected in the history and present day conflicts between the Islamic and Western worlds.

We argue that this tension and conflict are primarily derived from the repression of the feminine principle, thus relegating it to the cultural unconscious of the nations involved. According to Jung, the feminine principle is the knowledge that presides in the unconscious mind, the part of us that is unknown. In other words, both the Western and Islamic worlds have been dominated by a masculine oriented way of life. The feminine principle has then lived in the shadows of both cultures and has not easily been expressed for its own sake and, thus kept unconscious in both personal and collective psychology. We attempt, then, to integrate the personal and collective unconscious into consciousness with the hope of bringing our worlds a little closer through understanding. We can easily access the masculine part that is known to us but our actions often occur without the understanding of the psychology of the unconscious, the feminine aspect, that motivate that action. From a psychological perspective, *Lifting the Veil* calls for the emergence of the unknown aspects contained in the unconscious. Throughout this book, the veil is used as a symbol for what is hidden, what we do not know and urgently need to know.

The veil has emerged in the twenty-first century as an international symbol that holds a variety of meanings. The veil can be understood as merely the customary dress of Middle Eastern women, a religious expression, or a political statement. For some women donning the veil represents male dominance enforced by the threat of beatings or death, for others the veil signifies self-determination and independence in reaction to the threat of Western ideology impacting Islamic culture. The veil powerfully holds the polarity of attitudes and beliefs and invites the projections of the psychological complexes in both Western and Islamic societies. These negative shadow projections fuel external and internal conflict between and within each culture. The veil is not just a female garment to hide, protect, or humble Muslim women, but the curtain behind which resides the feminine principle, repressed in both East and West. Beneath the veil resides the unconsciousness of both cultures that become manifested in the politics of today.

To lift the veil of ignorance, it is necessary to understand both the Islamic and Western world views. Many Americans know virtually nothing about the history of the cultures, religions, and nations of the Islamic world. History classes in the United States are focused on American and European history and how Europe discovered, influenced, conflicted, and shaped American culture. The knowledge gaps, however, are wide about cultures other than European. Within that specific framework, everything the West knows about the world and its history tends to be viewed through a Western lens, influenced and molded within Christian ideology. All else is viewed as foreign and risks the possibility of being misunderstood since it seems different and is evaluated within our worldview.

The impact of 9/11 awakened our culture and brought a new awareness of our vulnerability. This event has challenged our perspective of ourselves, our culture, and our country, within the context of world conflict. The Western response to the tragic collapse of the World Trade Center and the Pentagon was filled with fear and revenge as our sense of safety and security dissolved. How do we see ourselves in response to 9/11? The American dream is the acquisition of material goods, the ideals of democracy, personal freedom, and technological achievement. We see ourselves as advent protectors of freedom heroically spreading freedom throughout the world. The image of freedom for all as well as liberating victims from tyrants and oppressors is contained in the one-sided view of the American cultural complex. The attack of 9/11 was an assault upon our fathers and their authority. The American culture was deeply traumatized, requiring defenses from deep within the cultural psyche to protect our profound wound. Most American knew little of Al Qaeda or why we were assaulted. We never asked about our contribution to the conflict but instead with the label of enemy, projected our own evil, primitive, and inferior aspects onto Al Qaeda. We identified with one side of the archetype, splitting off the negative side and attaching it to "them."

However, the Islamic culture, too, feels defeated and threatened after years of war between tribes and countries, Western colonialization and exploitation and the reality of globalization that threatens the stability of traditional Islamic society. Islamist figures have arisen as the archetypal defense of the collective wounded spirit.[1] Imaged by Osama Bin Laden, the *Mujahideen*, Khomeini, Arafat as well as the multitude of terrorist organizations, the characteristics of avenger and restorer become incarnated. The cultural memory of the lost *Caliphate*, world dominance and superior Islamic civilizations keep the longing to recreate the glory of a past time that compensates for the powerlessness felt today. The West becomes engaged as the rival defender of justice, freedom for all and God. Islamists protect the continuity and survival of Islam. The dynamics of cultural complexes are unleashed creating violence and destruction. All this hides behind the veil of righteousness and absolute truth.

---

1 Thomas Singer, "Cultural Complex and Archetypal Defenses of the Group Spirit: Baby Zeus, Elian Gonzales, Constantine's Sword, and Other Holy Wars." *The San Francisco Jung Institute Library Journal: Culture & Psyche*, Vol. 20 (2002), pp. 5-28.

Without a historical reference, the Islamic world is perceived through these kinds of Western projections, with little understanding of origin or direction. The unknown Islamic world is characterized, then, as a one dimensional black and white, right or wrong society, and judged within the limited scope of what is known to us and what we value. For this reason, we begin this book with an overview of Islamic history, trying to familiarize ourselves with some of the possible perceptions of the Islamic world which are shaped by their past. Jung offers a unique and helpful way to think about this conflict.

History provides the cultural conditioning which forms individual and cultural identity. In Jung's psychology, anything that threatens or conflicts with that ego position, whether it is the ego identity of an individual or a nation is called the shadow. The content of the shadow is mostly unknown and includes all the ideas and concepts that seem foreign and threatening to the ego or its identity. When the ego is threatened by the contents of the shadow, this content is projected outside of oneself onto another. The object of the projection is known as "the other." "The other" becomes a magnet for uncomfortable shadow projections casting all the negative darkness onto an unknown foreign person, place, or culture. Having a historical knowledge reduces the possibility of projecting shadow. History reveals common themes across cultures, emphasizing humanity's similarities.

Knowledge of history unfolds patterns as well as context. The conflict between the Christian and Islamic worlds, for example, did not start with 9/11 but are evident as far back as the Crusades. Although history is not stagnant but continuously moves forward, it also has a circular and repetitive motion—commonly referred to as "history repeating itself." All of history, all cultures, societies, and individuals have influenced each other over time and have borrowed from one another, exchanging ideas, technology, and genes. Therefore, the whole of humankind is all interrelated historically, not confined to its own time or place while constantly changing, interacting, destroying and creating.

Generally speaking, patterns in religion have swung widely throughout history between the strict and literal interpretation of Scriptures to these same Scriptures capable of flexible dialogue and observance. Political values have moved from individual freedom to authoritarian regimes and back again. Societies all over of the earth have dominated the world stage for periods of time, being the forerunners of change and/or the oppressors through conquest. Concepts such as humanitarianism and tolerance have flourished or been repressed over the centuries. Cultures, which have lived interdependently with a focus on human welfare and education, may regress to societies where isolation, prejudice, and militancy are the prevailing beliefs.

Although these ideas appear conflicting, according to Jung, they are really opposite sides of a polarity that represent the "whole." In other words, each side of cultural conflicting opposites both project shadow and are the recipients of shadow projections. Yet, these shadow projections, though dangerously exaggerated in content, carry elements of truth. The difficult task is to extract that truth which each projection carries. To whatever extent this is possible, the paradigm of innocence/guilt, victim/perpetrator dissolves. Individual human beings and cultural collectivities, according to this model, must strive for wholeness. For wholeness to exist, the shadow must be integrated into consciousness or ego. Therefore, at any given time or place within the framework of one side of the polarity, other alternative manifestations automatically exist that will compensate for the current view. Again, for example, if a person or culture leans too far to the masculine view of life, the feminine will have a compensatory demand to be accepted into the conscious worldview. Acceptance of both establishes a sense of wholeness. The integrated totality, which is a third non-polarized possibility, fills out the circle towards wholeness. The end result is neither a domination of one nor the other polarity but the union of both. The world, a nation, a culture, a society or an individual all contain conflicting parts, conscious or not, longing for integration against the forces of separation.

Each individual, then, represents a microcosm of opposing views and feelings that can be experienced as both positive and negative. To the Western worldview, the Islamic world frequently feels foreign and in opposition to a Western lifestyle. This Western shadow is projected onto the unknown "other," the Islamic world, which then accommodates us by relieving us of our responsibility for integrating that part of ourselves.

Our work as individuals, societies, and members of a world of humanity is to become more conscious. To that end, we need to understand ourselves psychologically both personally and within the context of our culture. We need to integrate the foreign parts that have been split off and demonized in the "other." This book hopes to direct our attention towards gaining that awareness. First, as mentioned above, we will try to give a concise overview of history that is relevant to the issues of today. Included is the making and falling of nations, the development of Islam and the economic influence as the world interconnects through the pressure of globalization. We introduce a psychological framework, described by Carl Jung, in which to view the individual within the world and then expand that paradigm by explaining the psychology of collective groups and societies. Using symbols that are bigger than life and that hold collective psychologies, we try to illustrate the dynamics presently being played out between the East and West. The book dances between archetypal images that express our common emotional views and experiences, on the one hand, and the facts that surround and feed the archetypal manifestations on the other.

We conclude with the image of Sheherazade, the hero, the image of wholeness and redemption of the feminine, who, single-handedly, lifts the veil to consciousness thus reintegrating all the lost parts. To integrate all the parts does not necessarily mean to transcend or evolve to a higher being or society. It is unknown how the world would look if all individuals or societies would take back shadow projections and tolerate differences. It may only mean that some individuals might expand knowledge of themselves by exposure and reaction to that otherness. To that end, this book is a journey of lifting the veil to what threatens our psyche and explore what is hidden.

PROLOGUE

A JUNGIAN PSYCHOLOGICAL APPROACH

The basic perspective used in our attempt to bring a deeper understanding of the cultural antagonisms and the historical bloody dramas that have been played out between the Western and Mid-Eastern world is psychology and Jungian psychology in particular. However, instead of applying Jungian theory to individual personalities as is the custom, this book applies it to cultures as though they are personalities in themselves. We will speak, then, of cultural "shadow," "archetypal" events, "anima" dramas, cultural "persona" overlays and cultural "projection" or cultural "complexes." One does not need to be a professional in the field of analytical psychology to understand these concepts as they are used here in their most general way.

For example, one of the more easily understood Jungian concepts is that of "persona." Increasingly today, one hears this term being applied to how anyone first encounters a person who relates in a predictable manner. For example, a police officer who has a difficult time taking his/her uniform and badge off at the end of the day and, instead, takes this identity home to his family, or relates, in the same manner, to his friends and himself, is caught in an over identification with the persona. If, however, he/she wears this persona as a protection on the job, his/her personal identity is appropriately protected when, for example, making an arrest. If he/she knows he/she is taking on the role of a police officer and does not hang his/her identity on it, the persona has served him/her to be more effective on the job. At the end of the day, the persona surface mask can be left at work. Basically then, the persona is the outer identity we show

9

the world in order to live appropriately and safely in it. It protects us from the world and the world from us. It is the ego's shield.

By ego we mean that field of consciousness we know about ourselves at any given time. It is the "I" that knows itself to be. It is what we know about ourselves now, and what we can recall about our personal history. Having an ego is different from being egotistical. Egotistical implies self-centeredness; thinking primarily of oneself or being blatantly selfish. To have an ego, an "I," is different. We need that in order even to have a relationship with the world around us. Who am I? – Where am I? – What am I? – Why am I? All these are a part of our ego awareness and the struggle to further define these questions. Ego is the heart of anything we know consciously. It is this that needs to be protected by the persona simply because the questions and their answers are so very personal.

Everyone needs a persona, in fact, most have more than one. Just as we need to dress the body, we need to dress our way of being to make ourselves adaptable to the world and, at the same time, to protect ourselves from the world. We wear the covering of our professions, our religious and political views, and relationships. The persona is like the skin on our personalities that helps us adapt to the world and the world to us. It is important to remember that while the persona serves to present how we are to be in the world, it is not reflective of our whole personality. We are not to identify with it. To do so, leads to a loss of life's deeper meaning and a world of superficialities.

When persona is applied to a collective level, it gets even more complicated because the persona identities have been built up over centuries and become deeply ingrained in the collective psyche. It is inevitable, therefore, that in the Western world we see people from the Middle East through our own personal identities to which we have become attached. In a parallel way, they respond to us from their persona identities. This culminates in two important areas of the world seeing each other through their limited understanding not only of the other but of themselves. The refusal of each side to look more deeply into the underlying cultural dynamics reflected in their differences in racial, religious, political, and social mores and to see beyond the surface prejudices, prepares the ground for terrible international relationships and superficial ways of handling conflict. Each culture becomes veiled under its persona. It is the veil that threads itself throughout this book becoming its central theme.

If the persona protects us from the world, it can also, through over identification, keep us from seeing the world and ourselves. Here is where the shadows lie, a term coined by C.G. Jung. Shadow refers to contents within our unconscious that go against how we see ourselves. If we see ourselves as morally solid and even somewhat self-righteous, the shadow of this would be reflected in our behaviors, fantasies and dream life revealing just how unaware we are of the immoral and un-righteous impulsive desires of which we do not think we are capable. The shadow could also be the reverse of this where rather immoral people would hardly imagine they are capable of doing a humanitarian act.

In the realm of shadow are, also, all those thoughts, potentials, fantasies, ideas, talents, and pre-dispositions that are not yet realized and accepted into the world of consciousness. They have not found a place consciously in the life of the individual which would in the end serve to make that person's life richer and wiser. To become more aware of our darker shadow side makes us less prone to judgment, more open to people of different backgrounds, more accepting and forgiving. We would realize that the very thing of which we would either demonize or idealize our neighbor is a part of our own personality structure.

In the collective shadow, the stakes are higher than on an individual basis, the dramas are costlier and the resolutions more difficult. The energy behind the collective shadow is the fuel that drives our wars, justifies our racism, and deadens our imaginations for peacemaking. Cultural/collective shadows blind us from understanding the history, ours and theirs, that has been played out to bring us to where we are today as well as how our own brand of understanding and interpreting history supports our bias toward the other. What we do not know about ourselves, we will project onto another. It is easier to see shadowy political machinations in the Middle East, for example, than to struggle with the same issues in the West. This is one of the core issues expounded on throughout this book.

One of the unique contributions of Jung was his concept of anima. Though originally, it was meant to signify a man's feminine side, and still does to a great extent, we can, also, speak of the feminine side in any number of things be it a person, an institution, or a nation. But what do we mean by the "feminine"? Like its counterpart, the "masculine," both have been subject to countless definitions, prejudicial descriptions, social distortions, and political manipulations. Yet, they do convey a reality that reflects deep layers in the human psyche of every person worldwide and are best mirrored in the worlds of religion, philosophy, and depth psychology. Though they include the sexual labels of "male" and "female," the words "feminine' and 'masculine' are far more inclusive and belong to everyone.

In the ancient Chinese Taoist worldview, for example, all of life is understood as the interplay of the Yin (feminine) and Yang (masculine) energies. These terms philosophically describe forces in the world around and within ourselves that balance and interplay upon each other. Yin is that which holds, receives, contains and births. It is darkness, earth, nature and carries the negative pole of existence. Yang is that which is light, heaven, spirit, active, expanding, penetrating and carries the positive pole of life. Trying to understand these two energies of life from the perspective of the Western way of thinking, can expose our prejudices when it comes to thinking, for example, that light is better than dark, positive is better than negative, heaven better than earth and so forth. If we understand these forces as a required balancing of each other and essential for the dynamic unfolding of life, then judgments must be suspended. The simple example of an electrical current demonstrates that both negative and positive poles are required to illuminate a light bulb. When both are in harmony, life functions in a healthy and balanced manner. When one dominates the other, discord ensues. Then, again, if there were no Yin and Yang energies, there would be no life.

These transpersonal and philosophical concepts take on practical expressions in the everyday lives of all of us. We can speak and have spoken, for example, of a masculine oriented culture where most everyone is affected by masculine ideas and approaches to life. Rarely do we speak of a feminine oriented culture. Yet, the feminine is there. Anima is what animates, brings life, stirs the imagination and favors life over rules and regulations and wants inclusivity and wholeness to predominate. Both masculine and feminine energies are important, but they must stay in balance like the Tao idea of Yin and Yang. Too much of one over the other and things go awry.

The political issues between the Middle East and the West have a lot to do with the repression of the feminine principle in both women and men and in both areas of the world. Certainly this repression of the anima is felt literally by women in some countries of the Middle East, for example, who are forced to wear a veil against their will or under other circumstances forbidden to wear it even if they want to. In North America, this repression may not look so dramatic but it takes only a minute understanding of our history to know how women have played a minimalist role in politics, business, and the international world scene. It affects everything we do in determining our approach to life in a more whole and balanced manner. The repressed feminine means an individual, nation, or culture is also repressed and stuck in a way of life that defies growth and creative new perspectives of how to move into the future. How different it would be if the energies behind masculine archetypal energies that are so directed to a fascination with war and military buildup were directed toward the archetypal feminine in causes like the environment, raising worldwide educational standards, population control and health care. These issues are not solely directed to men and women but to the psycho-spiritual forces that live in all of us.

We have said that when a psychological perspective is moved from the individual to the collective, it gets more complicated and difficult to resolve. But then what unites us as a world community? Jung's concept of the "archetype" suggests the common ground we all share. Just as the human body responds to basic instincts so does the psyche. In other words, as the instincts are to the body, the archetypes are to the psyche. An archetype is the psychological blueprint we all share that predisposes us to think and behave according to basic patterns regardless of where we live in the world. A simple way of saying this is that people everywhere are basically the same in terms of psychological patterns. The emotions accompanying birth, growing into adulthood, marriage, child rearing, aging, and death are familiar to everyone. Though cultural behavior may look and even be different around the world, the archetypal dynamics upon which such behaviors rest are the same everywhere. The details may vary as to how they are honored, ritualized and carried out, but the archetypal force behind them remains the same.

It is appropriate then to say that the anima and the shadow are archetypal forces being lived out everywhere in the world. When these forces are brought into politics, the weight of the archetype behind the cultural shadow/anima dynamics becomes monstrous, propelling us from one bloody conflict to another. Until the impersonal archetypal forces that live in us personally and collectively as nation states can be recognized and understood and then responsibly managed in the conscious and personal human realm, there is no hope in reconciling this or any other conflict.

It seems then that the only way out of this dilemma either individually or collectively is to courageously strive to incorporate into our understanding of ourselves that which is left out and most likely projected onto another. A sense of the "whole" must be established consciously with all the integrity and required honesty possible. In this regards, Jung developed his notion of a central complex that carries the idea of the "whole" which he called the Self, but not Self in the ego sense, that is, myself, yourself, ourselves, etc. His idea of the Self is the ultimate symbol of wholeness possible to the human race in that it holds both unity and totality. Nothing is to be left out which especially means our enemy. The best way to end the battle with the enemy is to look at that enemy within ourselves. As outrageous and naïve as this may be, if nation states would reflectively struggle to integrate within themselves, would try to understand the whys and wherefores of their shadow projected enemies, everything would change from how they did their politics to how they negotiated with their adversary.

The Self includes the ego, the persona, the anima/animus complexes—all the archetypal forces that live within every human being. Perhaps the greatest visible symbol we have for all peoples of the world regardless of race, religion, culture, or economic status is the photo of the Earth sent back to us from the moon so many years ago. The circle or the globe is the complete expression of the Self as we would know it because no thing, no person, no nation, no culture, or religion is left out. These and more go into making up this most earthly symbol of the Self.

Striving toward wholeness is part of the psychic structure of every human being and, by association, is integral to every nation and culture in as much as it is willing to strive toward ever greater levels of civility. The dilemma, however, is that the awareness of and resistance to the informing and integrating function of the Self in both the individual and collective psyche is resisted. Simply put, it is hard work to surrender our firmly held ego ground to open up to other possibilities that the world around and within ourselves has to offer. To experience that felt sense of the Self is to become aware that we stand in relationship with all humanity and that the long history of the human race and the wisdom it carries lives in us. It is this kind of consciousness of the whole that is mandatory as we move into the twenty-first century.

THE SELF

CONCEPTS	SHADOW	EGO
PERSONA	Cultural identifications, e.g., beliefs, freedom, democracy, and values. With the misuse of the shadow of power, each of these can take on sinister results.	The "other" is seen as holding anti-values and is a threat to a way of life that is so very consciously valued.
COMPLEX	A nation's or culture's story which includes its conscious history but also an unconscious shadowy history it does not know.	Stories of other people conflict with our stories. Thus "they" become the antagonist. If the ego is who we are, then the shadow is who we think we are not.
ARCHETYPE	Shared by all cultures. Here are found the patterns of cultural behavior	Shared by all cultures Here are found the patterns of cultural behavior

The above diagram illustrates the psychological concepts as described above as well as the interaction or dynamic between the concepts causing conflict within the whole. The idea of whole is used here meaning whole person, whole nation, or whole world. The whole, as a complete structure, is represented by what can be seen, the persona, the face shown to the world. The persona is the most conscious aspect of the psyche, the way we interact with other parts inside and out. The ego is the conscious mechanism that believes it is in control of the whole, the part that makes decisions and has opinions about others and ourselves. The ego is our identity, the part we call "I." The rest of the psyche resides in the unconscious, beginning with the shadow. Here are the aspects of ourselves we do not see or accept. Because of this, the shadow threatens the ego's sense of Self and well-being. Predictably then, the ego defends itself by projecting the shadow outside of itself onto an "other" person or nation.

Deep within the personal and collective unconscious psyche reside the complexes. A personal or cultural complex tells our individual or collective story and, therefore, shapes how the world is seen by each of us. These world stories differ everywhere. We need only to see today the growing antagonism between the United States and Mexico or between the Middle East and the Western powers, between China and Japan, North and South Korea, not to mention the differing nations of Africa. When our world story conflicts with another's world story, we are then faced with the decision regarding our relationship with the other based either on tolerance or antagonism.

The energy and drive in life is propelled through our complexes that, at the core, are fueled by universal archetypal patterns. These patterns are like dynamic energy systems inside us. Instead of fueling the body, however, they fuel our entire psychic world. Without them, we might not even be able to get out of bed in the morning or go about our daily business. As instincts drive the body, archetypes drive the psyche and reflect the basic motifs of life from beginning to end. These psychological dynamics reflect themselves in both individual and collective ways.

Individuals identify with the positive aspects of the cultural complex and project the negative parts onto another culture. The shadow carrier is perceived in an exaggerated negative manner of the unexplored shadow that remains unconscious in the psyche of the projector. In that way, the cultural ego identity is not threatened by the negative material contained within the whole archetypal energy and, thus, can continue to see itself as the hero, victim, or other innocent force in the narrative. Today, in much of Western and Islamic worlds, each group carries the shadow of the enemy and believes their existence is dependent on conquering the other.

The circle in the diagram on page 16 that contains the rectangle of individual parts is called the Self. The Self is the whole that wants both stories together having the same weight and importance. The whole of the individual, nation, and world are all the parts, not just the acceptable parts. The unacceptable splits off parts need to be incorporated and integrated into the whole. The struggle of bringing what is unconscious to consciousness is a commitment all individuals and nations must make. We conclude this chapter with this quote from C.G Jung:

> Our personal psychology is just a thin skin, a ripple on the ocean of collective psychology. The powerful factor, the factor which changes our whole life, which changes the surface of our known world, which makes history, is collective psychology, and collective psychology moves according to laws entirely different from those of our consciousness. The archetypes are the great decisive forces; they bring about the real events, and not our personal reasoning and practical intellect. The archetypal images decide the fate of man.[2]

Our own veil

2 Carl Jung, *Psychological Types*, CW 6, (New York, NY: Pantheon Books Inc, 1960), ¶. 183. NOTE: CW refers throughout to the *Collected Works of C.G. Jung*.

THE SYMBOL OF THE VEIL

The secrets eternal neither you know nor I
And answers to the riddle neither you know nor I
Behind the veil there is much talk about us, why
When the veil falls, neither you remain nor I.

Omar Khayyam

Still residing in my mind's eye after 45 years is the vision of an Arab woman standing on the top of a hill in the desert, her black robes being blown by the wind as the night approached. We watched each other from afar. I was struck by the beauty and grace of her image. There was no way to know her or her experience of life. Hidden under the robes that concealed her body was a world unknown to me. She resonated with a deep part of my soul and has remained on the periphery of my awareness. She has always been there and still calls to me today.[3]

If all humans are intertwined and enfolded into a whole, then any part of the species which is oppressed or potentially annihilated would pose a threat to the remaining parts by weakening the whole. According to Jung, the same principle holds true for the integrity of the psyche. Every possible psychic manifestation exists somewhere within one whole psyche, within every issue. We all have the possibility of being any "other" which resides in our unconscious. All

---

3 Jane Kamerling, co-author.

humanity resides within us as we are a part of all humanity. If we dissociate or ignore one part of ourselves, our whole psychology becomes vulnerable. The individuation path brings to consciousness what has been previously unconscious. The whole world is a part of me.

Islamic women's clothing has come to represent in the West, the otherness of Islamic culture. The same thing holds true of Western women's attire, both holding otherness for each corresponding culture. This otherness is seen as portraying the negative aspects of each culture. Therefore, the dress of the Islamic woman which will be unpacked later in this writing signifies primitive rigidity to the Western culture as the Western fashion connotes promiscuity and lack of rules to the Islamic culture.

Islamic women and their dress, as imaged above, have become the focus of world attention, not merely as a gender issue, but for broader political and cultural matters on the world stage. Specifically, the dress of Islamic women has come to represent repression and oppression of the female gender and the psychological feminine principle. The feminine principle defined as our unconscious selves, we consciously choose to ignore. What is ignored we see in the "other." The look of today's woman expresses a variety of values. Focusing on Islamic women, what a woman wears or does not wear symbolically expresses the voice of the presiding Islamic government, the established Muslim community, and the patriarchy. Western attitudes identify the attire of Muslim women as an expression of repression, oppression, and male dominance by a backward and primitive people. This book uses the veil as a metaphor of the unseen influences that affect the political and cultural world we live in. It represents both the actual oppression and abuse of women worldwide as well as the repression of unconscious material. This book emphasizes that the oppression of the feminine is both East and West, although, the veil is literally worn by women in the Islamic world. The veil, as a garment, is not the issue, but what it has

20

come to represent in the West through Western misunderstanding and misinterpretation.

Women may, however, choose to wear the veil in the Islamic world for several other possible reasons, such as signifying solidarity, nationhood, Islamic purism, resistance, liberation, feminism, anti-feminism, anti-globalization, theocracy, anti-colonialization, anti-imperialism, protection, modesty, religion, as well as, just for cultural tradition. The veil, therefore, emerges today as a powerful symbol containing political and cultural opposites provoking the whole world to concentrate on the image rather than the woman beneath the image. As is illustrated in the previous chapter on Jung's theoretical schema, the veil sets the border between the conscious and unconscious components of the psyche. Wearing the veil presents a cultural persona of Islam to the outside world. Yet, what is hidden beneath the veil is the unknown, or, in psychological language, the complexes and archetypes that fuel the whole personality. The veil, the barrier to awareness, crosses the borders between East and West whether seen as the literal donning of the veil or as a metaphorical image of unconsciousness. What follows is the exploration of the concrete, historical expression of Islamic women's dress in custom and law as well as "unconsciousness" and its implications in the world at large.

The Islamic tradition of the veil began when Muhammad, the prophet and founder of Islam, recited the words of Allah, in the *Koran*;

Tell the believing women to lower their eyes,

guard their private parts, and not display their charms

except what is apparent outwardly,

and cover their bosoms with their veils

and not to show their finery

except to their husbands or their fathers or fathers-in-law,

their sons or step sons, brothers, or their brothers' or sisters' sons, or their women attendants or captives,

or male attendants who do not have any need (for women),

or boys not yet aware of sex."[4]

Muhammad instituted the wearing of the veil. The donning of the veil is a pre-Islamic tradition from Persia that distinguishes upper class women and nobility. Mohammad adopted this form of fashion to honor his wives. From a practical perspective, covering his wives protected them from the masses of men that came to the Kabba to worship where his wives were living. As the *Sunnah*, the collection of the traditions practiced by the prophet, became the blueprint of Islamic custom and law, the wearing of the veil became a part of the traditional dress for women as well as a visible barometer which measures political/religious sentiment within Islamic society.

Over the last 1400 years of Islam, different centuries and places of Islamic practice have interpreted the above Sura along a spectrum from a strict to a more liberal dress code. How ironic that the garment which brings visibility to a philosophy of life is primarily designed to keep the female invisible. An observant Muslim woman covers herself so that she does not inspire sexual thoughts or actions among marriageable men, according to the teaching of the *Koran*. The stricter the Islamic law observed within her country, the more she is covered.

Islam requires *hijab*, a women's dress that follows Islamic principles. Literally, *hijab* means curtain, the divide between males and females, women and the world. Living behind the veil cuts off a woman's access to men outside her family and makes it difficult to interact in the public world, thus relegating her to the private world of her home. She lives behind the curtain and, when she moves, the curtain moves with her. Her ability to negotiate her life becomes limited and is dependent on the political agenda of her nation and/or

---

4 *The Koran, Sura*: 24:31.

her family's religious affiliation. Women are equal to men before God but legally inferior. *Hijab* in the Islamic world is both visible and literal and is imposed on women and men all over the world. The curtain is drawn, repressing the feminine principle that incorporates the idea of wholeness including what is not known or in the unconscious.

The feminine is feared in the Islamic world, as well as deeply repressed in the psyche of the Western world. Female and feminine have become synonymous. The fear of the feminine translates into man's fear of the woman. Females have been controlled by a fearful patriarchy through laws, religion and even dress. Leila Ahmed, in her book *Women and Gender in Islam*, writes how the West's discomfort with feminine issues resulted in a strategy of diverting Western attention to the Middle East in regards to oppression of women and antifeminism, during the period of colonialization in the Middle East and Africa.[5] This tactic served a dual purpose to undermine the Islamic culture as well as to redirect the feminist issues from the West Eastward. Looking at earlier Jewish and Christian cultures, both the foundation of Islam, women are given second place status to no status at all. The stories in the Old Testament generally give women a supporting actor role to the patriarchs and, in Christianity, God incarnates a masculine image.

The customary articles of dress within the Islamic world are called by a variety of names specific to particular nations. An example is a *Chador* that is a square piece of fabric which falls from top of the head to the ankles held or pinned closed under the chin, leaving only the face and hands visible. A chadris is also a full covering adding latticework over the eyes popular in Afghanistan, Lebanon, and Iran. An *abaya* is a variation of a coat like a black cloak with arm slits covering the head to the ankles preferred by the Persian Gulf

---

5 Leila Ahmed, *Women and Gender in Islam* (New Haven & London: Yale University Press, 1992).

countries. The *burca*, a garment Americans have heard so much about since the war in Afghanistan, is a facemask except for the eyes. By contrast, women in Pakistan wear silky tunics over pants with long shawls of matching fabric designed for comfort and mobility. The degree of cover depends on the nation in which one lives. The extent of concealment measures the strictness of Islamic interpretation and the everyday restrictions of the woman who wear them.

Along with *hijab*, the veil connotes the concept of seclusion. In Sura 24:31, Muhammad delineates which men are permitted to see a woman out of Islamic dress; these are men she can never marry and, therefore, they should not have lustful feeling towards her.[6] Other family members such as uncles or cousins, or family friends, or strangers can only be with her fully covered. In Sura 33:53, Muhammad, when describing how guests should behave in a man's house, states: "And when you ask his wife for something of utility, ask for it from behind the screen. For this is the purity of your hearts and theirs."[7] This Sura is the template for the separation of women from men, secluding women to a separate part of the house, called purda, living in quarters called the *harem* with other women of the household. The *hijab* and the *harem* hide the face of the woman. She has no voice. She is invisible.

Just as a woman finds herself vulnerable and powerless because she is hidden from the world, so too is an individual ego powerless to the unknown aspects of the unconscious. Unexplored complexes can cause conflict for the ego as, for example, when the ego discharges its unknown shadow side by projection onto the "other." In other words, whatever conflicts with the ego's image of itself will be seen as a problem belonging to someone else. Extrapolating this complex onto a culture, the culture defends against what it represses by projecting its shadow onto a corresponding "other."

6 *The Koran, Sura* 24:31.
7 *The Koran, Sura* 33:53.

The Islamic woman of today is caught in political divisions which both elevate her status as the center of the debate and, at the same time, limit her possibilities. Pluralism represents a threat to a culture that focuses on homogeneity and divine, unquestionable truth. Women represent differentness, the other. Understanding this, one of the first declarations of Ayatollah Khomeini after the Iranian revolution in 1979, was commanding women to veil. Veiling women reinstates Islamic law, imposing restrictions on women to appease men's discontent in the midst of political upheaval and temporarily to alleviate economic distress in countries where women live in seclusion and are forbidden to work. The result is control over women within a patriarchal culture where men dominate. Women, the feminine principle, and the repressed unconscious all share the same fate of cultural oppression. All three are used interchangeably in this book.

Yet, wearing the veil also signifies dignity, and for some women, it is a sign of resistance to Western domination. Women are pulled between political forces to which they are strongly identified and the feminist issues which impact their lives. To veil, which expresses a strong political statement and Islamic authenticity, can also trap women in a custom that reduces her personal liberation and power. However, to support feminist theory based on a Western model is seen as connected to Western ideology and therefore rejected. Therefore, to perceive the veil as a symbol of misogyny is felt as a loss of identity and autonomy. The tension between these opposite poles is held in the symbol of the veil. Some women have to prioritize which values are presently more meaningful. For others, their men have already made the decisions. The holistic attitude is to be aware of both interpretations incorporating the totality of possibilities.

Women symbolize their commitment to Islam by the way they dress. A woman represents her family, community and government. The honor of her family resides in her modesty and chastity. The discrepancies of power imposed through strict *hijab* and seclusion put women in a position of vulnerability. Passages from the *Koran* are used to validate God's intention of keeping women powerless and dependent on the benevolence of men. Women are expected to be obedient. "As to those women on whose part you fear disloyalty and ill-conduct, first admonish them, then refuse to share their bed, and last beat them, but if they return to obedience, do not seek a way against them."[8] The *Koran* goes on to say that women "have the same right as is exercised over them, though the men have a rank above them."[9] Islam tries to give women more rights than predecessors of rival tribes and peoples, but, in the end, the authority resides with the males.

The *Haddith*, which are the traditions and sayings of Muhammad, re-emphasizes the role of women as subjugated to the commands of men. Muhammad says that the "whole world is delightful, but the most delightful thing in it is a virtuous woman."[10] She is a good woman if "She pleases him when he looks at her, obeys him when he commands, and does not oppose him in things which he rejects for her and for himself."[11] He becomes descriptive of her role when he states, "If it is proper for a human being to kneel in adoration of another human being, then this is only for a woman to kneel to a man."[12] Muhammad saw the need to control women because of the threat he perceived existed toward men. "I have left behind no temptation more harmful to my community than that which women represent to men."[13] The danger implied is male's loss of control over himself and his family due to his sexual needs. Woman

---

8 *The Koran, Sura* 4:34.

9 *The Koran, Sura* 2: 228.

10 *Haddith* 82, II, 168.

11 *Haddith* 82, II, 168.

12 *Haddith,* 82, II, 25.

13 *Haddith* 120, VI, 411.

represents pleasure and the fulfillment of man's sexual desire. The male needs to dominate the object of his need. This domination is also seen as protection. This ancient attitude of tribal men living in a dangerous time of chaos and continual tribal wars is literally interpreted today as the word of God for behaviors appropriate for the twenty-first century. For extremists, the *Koran*, *Haddith*, and *Sharia* (Islamic Law) gives license for misogynist behaviors towards women.

Family members kill women whose virtue has been questioned. These murders are called honor killings. Brothers have killed their sisters in order to spare the family humiliation and assure the marriage of other female children. Women are burdened to uphold men's honor and sexuality by dressing modestly, covered, and casting their eyes downward. They are not to excite or stimulate a man's sexuality. In Iran, there are frequent signs that state, "For respect of Islam, *Hijab* is mandatory." The penalty of "bad *hijab*" is one to twelve months in prison or flogging or paying a fine per lash of flogging.[14] In some countries women cannot leave their home without the permission of their husbands and then may only visit relatives, the cemetery, the market, hear prayers by a holy man, or attend a celebration for a religious holiday in a mosque. Today, in Saudi Arabia, women cannot be seen in a restaurant or go to the movies. Women need to be driven; they are not permitted to drive and must be accompanied by a man in public. In most Islamic countries, women cannot leave the country without their husband's consent.

In Pakistan there is a wave of dowry burnings, which is the burning of wives by their husbands because they want a higher dowry than was originally agreed upon. Men blackmail the families of their brides to extort money by threatening to burn the women. If the families have little or no money, the wives are burned to death or divorced and cast out with serious bodily burns and no possibility of

---

14 Ahmed, p. 109.

future marriage. A woman living outside of marriage in the Islamic culture can be easily exploited and/or disenfranchised.

These customs and abuses happen in countries where women have little or no voice. It is difficult to negotiate with the outer world if you cannot be seen or heard. They are veiled, secluded, and in some cases exploited and abused. Here the concretization of the psychological repression of the feminine principle is manifested in the lives of Muslim women. In Pakistan an estimated eighty percent of women suffer domestic violence as reported by Sally Armstrong in her book, *Veiled Threat*.[15] She also points to the rise of women in prisons due to the harsh and unfair Hudood Ordinances that were established in Pakistan in 1979. These ordinances, called Zina laws, govern adultery, fornication, rape, and prostitution. A woman can be accused of prostitution, fornication, or adultery when she has, in fact, been raped. In September 2006, due to Western pressure, Pakistan amended the Hudood laws with a Women's Protection Bill. The Bill does not address the concerns regarding punishments the law prescribes which are inhuman, as well as the inability for women to be equally heard.[16] *Sharia*, Islamic law, considers a woman's word one half that of a man's in a court of law. A woman is presumed guilty and can only prove her innocence when four males state that she has, in fact, been raped or maligned. The Human Rights Commission of Pakistan reiterates its demand that the Hudood laws be repealed believing the Women's Protection amendment to be a political farce.

Women live in a substandard world where they are vulnerable within their culture and need to depend on the protection of her father, brothers, and husband. Mukhtar Mai, a poor Pakistani woman,

15 Sally Armstrong, *Veiled Threat* (New York, N.Y.: Random House, 2000), p. 76.

16 Asian-American Network Against Abuse of Women (ANAA) Panel discussion "Women's Rights and Muslim Communities - Honor, Culture, and Islam." Dr. Anna Buttar, President DePaul University, Chicago, July 16, 2005.

was publicly gang raped as retribution for the alleged transgressions of her preadolescent brother in June 2002. She contemplated suicide by swallowing acid but was deterred by her mother. Other women have not been fortunate enough to have families stand beside them, but rather sacrificed raped family members to honor killings. Other women, who have accused their perpetrators, lose the battle in Islamic court and are sometimes charged with Zina laws. Mukhtar Mai began to speak out about the injustices of the Pakistan legal system and attracted the attention of international journalists and human rights organizations. With worldwide support she was able to tell her story to the Supreme Court of Pakistan. October 2006, the publication of her book, *In the Name of Honor*, was released. Gloria Steinem writes, "Only a few leaders are alchemists who take the worst of human behavior and turn it into the best. Mukhtar Mai, a Pakistani woman raised in poverty and illiteracy has consistently responded to the violence and gender apartheid directed at her and other women with an insistence on justice and education."[17]

In July 14, 2005 in Pakistan, the MMA (legislative body of Pakistan) passed the Hasba Bill into law. Under this law, a moral police force was established so that Muslims would behave according to Islamic teachings in public places. Released to the press, the bill vowed to "introduce *Taliban* style of governance in Pakistan." The law also insures that all decisions made by the mostasib, or ombudsman, have complete authority to enforce their version of Islam. This law, in combination with existing laws, can only bring more oppression and abuse upon the women of Pakistan.

Taking custom and Islamic law to an absurd and sadistic extreme, the *Taliban* threatened and repressed the women of Afghanistan for a decade. Some of the edicts enforced on any female above the age of ten were as follows: Translated by the United Nations (Sally Armstrong *Veiled Threat*):

---

17 Mukhtar Mai, *In the Name of Honor* (New York, N.Y.: Atria Books, 2000).

- No exit and traveling of sisters without escort of legal close relatives.
- Those sisters are coming out of their homes with legal escort should use veil (*burca*) or similar things to cover the face.
- Sitting of sisters in the front seat of cart and Jeep without legal relative is forbidden.
- Shop keepers do not have the right to buy or sell things with those women without covered face.
- Women's invitations in hotels and wedding party in hotels are forbidden.
- Sisters without a close relative with them cannot use taxis . . .
- Female patients should go to see female physicians. In case a male physician is needed, her close relative should accompany the female patient.
- During examination, the female patients examined by male physicians should be dressed with an Islamic *Hijab.*
- Sitting and speaking between male and female doctors is not permitted. If there is need for discussion, it should be done with *Hijab.*
- Staff of religious police departments are allowed to go for control at any time and nobody can prevent them. Anybody who violates the order will be punished as per Islamic regulations.[18]

Women were not allowed to work, go to school, wear make up, nail polish or jewelry. Everyone was banned from listening to music, keeping or playing with birds, flying kites, or laughing. This sounds like a sadomasochistic novel. However, distorting the meaning and intention of Allah's name and teachings, the *Taliban* was able to institute complete control over Afghanistan by terrorizing its people with violence and torture. Most of the edicts were directed at women, calling for strict *hijab* and seclusion. Through the suppression of a woman's freedom, the government dominated the lives of everyone. Women were dominated by the laws themselves which

---

18 Armstrong, *Veiled Threat,* pp. 12-17.

regulated their ability to interact within their culture. Men were dominated by the fear of harm to their women and the need of their protection. Men, therefore, had the additional responsibilities for the safety of their mothers, their sisters, their wives, and their daughters.

In contrast to the enforcement of external rules, such as imposed by the *Taliban*, some women living in other places throughout the world are choosing, of their own accord, Islamic dress and men are voluntarily affiliating with Islamist groups. Studies indicate that these men and women are young and educated. Men are typically between the ages of seventeen and twenty-six while women are usually older. Both men and women are attending or attended university and study subjects that require high intelligence. Most are from lower or middle class rural backgrounds or come from families that have recently moved to cities. These young people are upwardly mobile, confronted by stresses of high goals, in cities filled with consumerism, materialism, and foreign presence. They are choosing Islamic dress and Islamic movements as a coping strategy that rejects Western dress, secularism, feminism, and Western ideology and, at the same time, affirming and restoring traditional values keeping stress at bay. Rather than being seen as regressive or repressive, this new generation of women feel autonomous in a new way of negotiating within the Islamic world.

Islamic feminists see this trend as authoritarian, male dominated, and misogynist.[19] In a culture that has no tolerance for ambiguity, some feminists work to reinterpret political, governmental and legal systems, rejecting veiling and the Islamic movements as perpetuating an already unbalanced power base. In validation of the feminist perspective, the World Bank released a report stating, "Societies that discriminate on the basis of gender pay a significant price in greater poverty, slower economic growth, weaker governance, and a lower

Women ≠ equal in West either

---

19 Ahmed, pp. 221-225.

Western vs. Islamic
morally corrupt — tyrannical

quality of life."[20] Individuals and cultures pay a high price through the oppression and repression of the feminine (female) principle. Women are eliminated from contributing to economic and political dialogue within their society. Untapped female resources short-change the culture by eliminating fifty percent of its riches. All parts must be integrated and a dialogue established between men and women, East and West, the ego and the unconscious. The feminist call for liberation is not only a call from female oppression, it is also a call for the liberation of all peoples unconscious shadow material. The emergence of unconscious material leads to broader future possibilities.

Contained within the symbol of the veil opposites collide in a battle containing universal polarities where all peoples and cultures reside. Two cultures project degrading and destructive images on one another. The West is seen as morally corrupt, socially degenerate, nonintellectual, untrustworthy, passive, ungodly, soulless, and materialistic. The Islamic world is viewed as fanatical, rigid, backward, primitive, and aggressive. Issues clash, contradicting, locked in conviction, differing in position, struggling for dominance, unwilling to reconcile. Democracy versus theocracy, feminism versus antifeminism, modernization versus traditionalism, secularism versus spirituality, and globalization versus anti-globalization, all creating a tension of exploding forces that are enacted on the current world stage. Carl Jung warned that separation to the extreme when "carried so far that the complementary opposite is lost sight of, and the blackness of the whiteness, the evil of the good, the depth of the heights, and so on, is no longer seen, the result is one sidedness, which is then compensated from the unconscious without our help. The counterbalancing is even done against our will, which in consequence must become more and more fanatical until it brings

---

20 World Bank, December 6, 2001.

about a catastrophic *enantiodromia*.[21] Wisdom never forgets that all things have two sides, and it would also know how to avoid such calamities if ever it had any power. But power is never found in the seat of wisdom; it is always the focus of mass interests and is therefore inevitably associated with the illimitable folly of the mass man."[22] What is Jung trying to say? The more we project our cultural shadow on to the, "other" the more extreme each position becomes. The suffering of the shadow energizes the need to project its negativity outward, demonizing the other and raising the stakes of one's individual and cultural survival. Ultimately, this leads to extremism and war, "the illimitable folly of the mass man."

The feminine principle of relatedness, dialogue, and understanding resides under the layers of clothing worn to cover up and deny the unconscious. The psychological process needs to be exposed to reveal the dynamics of the Islamic and Western interactions and projections. The veil needs to be lifted to understand the cultural complexes of these two worlds, the archetypes that drive their actions, and the redemption of the feminine principle, as well as, women in patriarchal cultures.

---

21 *Enantiodromia* literally, "running counter to," referring to the emergence of the unconscious opposite in the course of time. see C.G. Jung, *Psychological Types*, "Definitions," CW 6, ¶ 709. "This characteristic phenomenon practically always occurs when an extreme, one-sided tendency dominates conscious life; in time an equally powerful counterposition is built up, which first inhibits the conscious performance and subsequently breaks through the conscious control."

22 C.G. Jung, *Mysterium Coniunctionis*, CW 14, (New York, N.Y.: Princeton University Press, 1956), ¶ 470.

33

OUR CULTURAL WOUNDS

FROM THE LONE RANGER TO SALADIN

One of the practical hallmarks in the study of the human personality was the discovery of depth psychology. Complexes reside under the veil, the veil being defined as the boundary between conscious and unconscious. When we use the word "complex" we can think of it in different contexts, but all of which hearken back to a common source of meaning. Someone could say: "It's a complex situation," or "He/She is a complex person," or "This matter is a complex of ideas." In every case, it is saying that there is more here than meets the eye, that is, something is beyond our conscious ability to see, understand and fully relate to the matter at hand. Something is hidden from us. Something lies in the background of our ability to fully or even partially grasp. In this sense, a complex is in the depths of the unconscious, and, though accessible, is multifaceted and hidden by our own defenses, protecting us from the dangerous world around us and locking us into the distorted stories we need to survive. Accordingly, our world is veiled both within and without ourselves, keeping us from our own personal and collective truths. It is used to keep us from internal threats and conscious insights. It also keeps us from seeing life as it is and prevents us from healing and growth.

A complex is an emotionally charged grouping of ideas, memories and images that cluster around a central core. For example, let us say the central core is that of mother or father. These themes carry an emotional charge that can make us feel positive or negative, warm or cold, happy or sad, and so forth. We can carry ideas about these themes, memories, and internal images that may or may not match up with the actual reality of these themes. Over the course of a lifetime, the notion of mother or father can expand to include anything, anybody, any idea or institution that carries their emotional charge. Or, take as another example, an early life trauma complex whether physical, emotional, or verbal. The complex behind such memories and automatic behavior reflexes is wounded—most often identified as a wounded child complex. Though many years and even decades have passed, an individual will predictably respond in the same wounded child complex behaviors when a memory stimulus is present. It is all unconscious and is designed to protect the individual from a perceived threat much as had happened when the individual was a child. These ideas, memories, and images are a part of our psychological world we either have repressed or are a part of the potential for our life that has not yet manifested. In either case, they are unknown or unconscious to us. Yet, they are very real and need to be taken seriously if they are not left to manifest in our lives in disturbing, embarrassing, or destructive ways. Even a rudimentary understanding of this basic psychological principle is critical for gaining a more expansive understanding of ourselves and our motives for thinking and acting the way we do. This is critical for understanding and healing the multitude of conflicts between people and the "complex" of relationships in which we can get tangled.

If we know what hidden triggers are pressed within us or the other, if we know about our once forgotten wounds or the wounds of another, our interactions might be quite different. If we are aware of such things even dimly, this creates the ethical task to respond differently. The task is to know what we do not know and to have the moral fiber to act in a manner that reflects this. We all have complexes which, over time, become the means by which we get to know ourselves. They are required for self-awareness. The task of psychotherapy, or analysis, or everyday self-reflection, however, is not to let them have us. Because of complexes, we have a unique opportunity to develop ourselves, to add to our field of self-knowledge and develop a more responsible and conscious approach to the world. Complexes are a part of the human condition and create the drama of our personal individuation journeys. Whether we talk about parental, child, power, shadow, initiatory, or religious complexes, they and others get played out over the course of a person's life. Each has an archetypal foundation peculiar to the human race which are the seeds that evolve into the stories that make up our personal journeys. For example, one only has to ponder how a mother or father complex either evolves in a person's life in such a manner that strengthens and wizens throughout a lifetime, or cripples a person's individuation process.

Yet, it is not only our personal individuation journeys that are of concern here. Complexes also take on more than a personal life. Institutions, organizations, cultures, and nation states can be like individual personalities having all the struggles and dramas of complexes peculiar to any one person. Complexes belonging to a culture have specific characteristics that have grown out of historical events, often of a painful nature. In recorded human history, the list of such events is exhausting. To study with some depth the history of any given nation is to study its complexes, what they are, how they got activated, how they manifested, and how they continue to grow or die away or get resolved. Herein is the value of remembering or keeping conscious our history lest we are doomed to repeat it simply because of complexes that remain unresolved in a state of cultural unconsciousness.

The painful clarity of this truth was most evident at the beginning of this twenty-first century in both the conscious political attitudes and unconscious projections of complexes between the Islamic and Western world—North America in particular. The question asked after the two Trade Towers in New York were leveled was: "Why do they hate us?" The question is understandable. Most of us in North America know little either of Islam as a religion nor of the fourteen hundred year history that saw its emergence from the desert oasis of Medina to a vast empire that included half of the known world. Neither were we aware that 1492 was not just the year Columbus, backed by Queen Isabella, stumbled upon America, but was also the year Queen Isabella instituted the Spanish Inquisition that expelled every Jew and Muslim from Spain unless they converted to Christianity. The final humiliation for the Islamic world came with the fall of the Ottoman Empire after World War I that resulted in the Western powers dividing up the lands of the Middle East. For North Americans, these historical events took place on the other side of the world, so how could we or should we be aware of the struggles of these diverse groups. At most, our interests were confined to Persian rugs, Arabian coffee, and most of all, oil. In contrast, Muslim communities do not forget their history. The cultural wounds centuries in the making created deep and long lasting cultural complexes waiting to erupt, saturated with longstanding feelings that were certainly felt personally as well as collectively.

The idea that cultures, like individuals, have complexes and can act like individual personalities, albeit of a collective nature, is new to the world of psychology. It is not for lack of studies about cultural differences and the impact this makes on individuals. What had not been clearly articulated until recently is the phenomenon of "cultural complexes" themselves.[23]

A concise statement of the notion that a culture is like an individual with its own peculiar set of complexes is reflected in any nations cultural complexes having their origins in its own unique cultural unconscious. It then interacts with not only the basic ways people act everywhere, but also with the specific personal expressions of the culture itself as seen, for example, in its politics, education, arts, work arena, religious life, and so forth. Though such things go to make up a culture, the personality of a nation is shaped by the events of its history that can often be violent, traumatic, and humiliating.

Putting this simply, as an individual can experience the devastating and debilitating effects of trauma for decades, a culture can suffer the severity of its history of violence for centuries. The history of violence peculiar to any culture might be known or not known to the individuals within that collective. Like people, nations might not even be consciously aware of what they suffer, or, conversely, they might be and act accordingly. Herein lay the primary dynamic that sets the stage for conflict between and within nations. An example is a nation or any collective group with longstanding historical wounds may act defensively to protect itself from future harm. This was reflected in the humiliation Germany felt after WWI paving the way for the horrors of WWII; or in the Iranian Revolution of

---

23 Thomas Singer and Samuel L. Kimbles, *The Cultural Complex: Contemporary Jungian Perspectives on Psyche and Society*, (New York, N.Y.: Brunner-Routledge, 2004).

humiliations (9/11 + Vietnam) affect our self view for years to come

1987 that reflected anger over the interference of Western powers; or in the eruption of African Americans in the 1960s for centuries of abuse; or in Native American's taking over the Bureau of Indian Affairs in Washington, D.C. in 1972 in order to have a voice in their own governance; or devout Muslims seeing the presence of military troops in Saudi Arabia as a violation and contamination of their religion. All of these were defensive acts intended to protect and preserve a way of life with its particular worldview.

When a cultural complex has been activated at the heart of a culture, predictable and basic human defenses of the group spirit rise up to defend the culture from further injury. The emphasis here is on "group spirit" because the wounding history belongs to everyone.[24] Just as when an individual finds him or herself under attack, a defensive position will be taken, so the same works for a culture. These predictable and understandable defenses continue so long as the violated and traumatized heart of the culture remains unresolved, contaminating both its conscious and unconscious life. This unfinished work can be either interjected into the life of the group itself, and/or projected out on other cultures resulting in further traumatizing through the horrors of wars and cultural prejudice.[25]

Because cultural complexes, by their nature, are collective, the force of their expression is most often sweeping in nature and horrific in effect, as we hear nearly every day from news reports. It takes a long time to change cultural complexes, because they are collective. Individuals change quicker than cultures for this reason, but the dynamics of complexes are the same in both realms. An individual, for example, has their own issues that

---

24 Singer, "Archetypal Defenses of the Group Spirit."

25 D. Kalsched, *The Inner World of Trauma: Archetypal Defenses of the Personal Spirit*, (London and New York: Routledge, 1996).

could be worked out over the lifetime of a few decades. A culture, by contrast, deals with collective issues that have often evolved over centuries, making change move slowly. It is one thing to face our personal complexes; it is another to face the cultural complexes that affect us. From the perspective of the individual, however, it is important to ask "what is living me?"— a question that might help depersonalize the emotional weight one is carrying, a weight that belongs to the greater collective be it family, work place, or nation and not solely to ones personal history.

With this perspective in mind, the question needs to be asked what the cultural complexes are of North America. It is here that one walks through a tangled maze with one complex flowing into another. They are expressed, of course, in racism, in growing class divisions, in educational disparities, in religion, in attitudes to land use (corporate versus ecological concerns), and in the extreme demonizing electoral processes between the red and blue. The list can go on, yet perhaps these cultural complexes may be the fallout of deeper wounds that have been with us as a nation for a long time. What is being proposed here in broad strokes is not any one answer for our cultural complexes but one consideration, one longstanding and very deep cultural veil.

That consideration takes us back five hundred years to when Europeans first stepped foot on this continent. They came as immigrants often on the run, disenfranchised from their own countries by choice or force or as adventurers or profiteers. They left the place of their ancestors, where their dead were buried. They left their living friends and relatives behind. They left the familiar streets, market centers, and places of worship. They left the motherland, the fatherland. These are relational terms that endear one to a place like a child of that land. These are terms that are not said of our country. We speak of North *interesting?*

America, America, the United States of America, or "my country tis of thee" but never as "motherland" or "fatherland." The closest we get are in the words "patriot" or "patriarchy" which have their roots in the Latin word, pater, for father. Even still, this reflects an impersonal, non-relative relationship that the American psyche has been affected by for most of its history. When Europeans came to these shores, they were not children of this land. They were people who needed to survive an unfamiliar territory and the unfamiliar peoples of this place. This need to survive turned eventually to a need to conquer, and mixed with religious motives, eventually turned into the doctrine of Manifest Destiny.

What is being suggested here is a core wound of grief and fear that have been with us from the beginning. The tremendous psychic loss for the separation from the homeland they left behind accompanied by the disconnect to the soul of a new land and the need to survive in a strange place set the ground later for perpetuating this collective grief on an unconscious level as to how we related to this land and its inhabitants. The land was an 'it' devoid of soul and the inhabitants were of the legion of Satan needing to be changed or eliminated. The template was now established. Now we had no mother, no father. We had to rely on ourselves through an individualism of domination, power, conquest, and ascendancy. Yet beneath this self-reliant conquestatorial attitude was and is the still unfinished business of our grief and fear. Now, unfortunately, what was once conscious grief has become deeply embedded in our unconscious collective psyche. This is because of our history of violation of the land, our treatment of the original native population, and not having our own Euro-indigenous past planted firmly enough in this soil. We do not speak here specifically of individuals but of the cultural collective unconscious. There are many who consciously suffer the effects of our violations against the land and against ourselves and others throughout our history. But psycho-dynamically, this unconscious collective grief that started so long ago is now compensatory to the American collective ego that seems to know no bounds in its need to secure itself materially and militarily on both a national and international level.

We do not see this collective grief because it is unconscious. It is veiled. Yet we find its symptoms in the agitations of our country, in our violence, our disconnect between youth and elders, our breakdown of families, and the feelings of loneliness and alienation so many feel because they do not belong. In short, there is an unconscious grief for the loss of deep community, for that universal sense of family with one another and for knowing the land as a living relative. This is more than a new age sentiment—it is fundamental to human beings worldwide.

What do we do with our grief as a nation when we do not know we are grieving? There are so many experiences that seem unfinished from all the wars in which we have participated, along with our own apartheids related to African and Native Americans, internments of American Japanese, etc., up to the present time. It has been stated that history is never past. It either lives in our conscious awareness or in our unconscious, but it is never past. The memories are there as food to feed our cultural complexes to be projected on other collectivities. Cultures have stories, or myths, that reflect these cultural wounds and complexes. These stories describe and often attempt to heal the problem.

Two such familiar stories from two different cultures stand out, one being non historical but quite mythical from North America and one historical that has taken on mythical proportions in Islam. It is to be understood that these are tens of thousands of stories that reflect these two cultures. Such stories should be seen as the dream life of a culture and are attempts to both express the problems of that culture and the key to their solutions.

In 1949 the adventures of the Lone Ranger and his companion friend, Tonto made its first radio broadcast. America became fascinated with the nightly continuing series of these two men, and generations later we still refer to them. What most people do not know is how the Lone Ranger became the Lone Ranger. Here is the short form broadcast of the very first night over radio to America.

There was a vicious outlaw group known as the Cavendish gang. Six Texas Rangers led by Captain Dan Reid, the Lone Ranger's brother, decide to go after them. They are aided by a half-breed Indian named Collins. Collins knows where the gang is and takes the Rangers down a canyon path to an area near the hiding place of the Cavendish group. What the Rangers do not know is that Collins is secretly working for the Cavendish gang led by Butch Cavendish. The end result is that all six Rangers are shot. After Collins determines they are dead, Butch kills him, believing if Collins could betray the rangers, he could betray him. After they leave, one of the rangers thought dead is very much alive and crawls to a nearby cave.

Shortly after, an Indian rides by, finds the ranger and recognizes a medallion around his neck as one he had given him when they were boys. "You, Kemo Sabe," the Indian says and reminds his friend that the Ranger had come to his rescue when his camp had been burned and his family killed when he was a young boy left to die. This Indian, Tonto, nurses the ranger back to health whereupon the ranger tells him, "I've been doing a lot of thinking. I'm going to devote my life to ridding the West of outlaws. But I'll need a disguise of some kind. I don't want any one to know who I am. Tonto makes him a mask and tells him he is alone now, a lone ranger to which his friend says, "Yes, Tonto, I am the Lone Ranger."

The story goes on from there to the Lone Ranger rescuing a beautiful silver stallion that he names Silver and having a friend make silver bullets for him. Now they are ready, the Lone Ranger on Silver and Tonto on Scout to head out as a team to rid the West of outlaws and bring in a day of justice.

In episode three, after the Cavendish gang is captured by them and brought to the local sheriff, Tonto says to his friend that he can now take his mask off. The Lone Ranger replies by saying, "No. I'm going to continue wearing this mask as long as there are outlaws in the West. I want to make this a safer place to live. Come on, Tonto, we've got lots of trails to ride." Inside the jail, Butch Cavendish turns to the sheriff and asks him who that masked man was. "I don't rightly know," says the sheriff, "but I heard the Indian call him the Lone Ranger." To which we hear, "Hi-Yo Silver Away."

If we treat the Lone Ranger/Tonto phenomenon like a cultural dream, then it is fair to suggest that the reason it caught the interest of so many Americans is because it touched something in the collective cultural unconscious that spoke to the need to heal the dissociation from the land as a living intimate reality and the native inhabitant as partners in this new cultural adventure. Consider, for example, the near equal relationship that exists between the Lone Ranger and Tonto. Tonto is no ordinary sidekick that usually accompanies a cowboy hero. He plays a serious role and, by his presence, suggests a partnering of two varying cultures, the European and Native views of life. But think of these two men as metaphors that transcend race or gender. It is essential to keep this before us if we are to understand the deeper impact of this cultural story. In contrast to the typical cowboy hero who rides off into the sunset, the Lone Ranger and Tonto represent what should have been a unification of all the best of what our Western culture stands for and can achieve working along side our own most fundamental indigenous heritage as human beings who are deeply allied with the earth and can speak for the wisdom that comes from it. The Lone Ranger and Tonto represent ways of being that are a part of all of us and, in the manner of dream work, are best treated as dream images in any one person or our culture as a whole.

The Lone Ranger as masked man falls into the same genre of hero figures as Zorro of Mexico, Batman, Spiderman or even Superman, all of whom did not want their identity to be known. It is a strange form of the veil theme that allows the deeper and purer motives of justice to evolve. The Lone Ranger/Tonto partnership is a metaphor of the archetype of justice uncontaminated with individual or cultural ego needs. Here, there are no political, racial, economic, or religious party lines to follow. There is no need for personal recognition. These figures just want the right thing done. We have here the hero figure in service to justice so that wrong can be righted and life can go on in the best way possible—a symbol of redemption.

Yet, fulfilling justice by righting the wrong can be taken two ways. Justice can be a two-edged sword. Most of us know of the one edge that demands what is often unreasonable and even inhuman obedience to the law. This is not justice here defined, it is simply the law. The idea of justice, in this sense, can be used to limit people's freedom, suppress opportunities of self expression, incarcerate people unfairly, and turn one group of people against another. Granted, these are extreme misuses of the law parading behind self-serving notions of justice. Yet, countries around the world, including what we know as enlightened first world nations, have had checkered histories of such political ideas of justice. Even softer expressions of justice that focus on the fulfillment of what are considered reasonable expressions of the law rather than the subtle circumstances behind events, can fail not only the deeper human levels of justice for an individual but for the greater community at large.

It is this greater embrace of justice that the Lone Ranger/ Tonto dedicate themselves to fulfill. The Lone Ranger is an untypical Western hero precisely because it is this hero motif with which he does not identify. He needs to wear a mask to hide his identity. He does not need to be a male hero, seeking recognition, status, and personal legend. Because he willingly lays aside a potentially inflated male ego, he makes room for the inclusion of a feminine embrace of justice as well. His need is anonymity which becomes also his requirement if any kind of personal identification and influence of justice is to be avoided. Archetypally toned ancient hero myths do not focus on the hero himself so much as what he or she, as true hero, does for the community he or she represents. The true hero is the one who commits him/herself to the community as a whole whether they appreciate him or her or not. The Lone Ranger and Tonto dedicate themselves to the feminine principle in that they are concerned about justice that takes the whole community into consideration. It is a principle that emphasizes relatedness within the entire human community. If injustice is done to one person, it is done to the community whether seen as a local aggregate of people or the entire world itself. It is no accident that statues of justice in our Western world are of a woman blindfolded. This must be seen only on an archetypal level in that the focus of the feminine principle is not in the laws, mores, and structures of a culture, but in the feelings and relationship one has to these laws, mores, and structures. A culture can have a law but not have the spirit of the law. Justice uncontaminated makes room for the latter.

Though, in the human realm, the ideas of pure justice are impossible to achieve, mythical figures support and remind us of the ideal standard of justice. The implementation of justice will always be influenced and contaminated to one degree or another by our cultural ego needs for good or bad. Though this is inevitable, there is also the serious need to constantly reflect on how to make the best expression of justice possible for ourselves and in our relationship to the world community.

After 9/11, the greater share of the world responded to our loss with concern and empathy. The trauma was overwhelming to the American psyche. It did not take long, however, for the basically human defensive reaction of the group spirit in the United States to take over. We quickly dissociated and projected our political shadow motives with a Lone Ranger energy believing we were bringing justice to the Middle East. But it was not justice for the sake of justice but, rather, retaliation in the form of vengeance. It was justice American style. This all happened because we did not grieve our trauma fully with all the understanding and reflection this requires.

It did not take long for the world to see through our motives. Nor did it take long to declare war and invade Iraq. The Lone Ranger lost the mask that represented his pursuit of pure justice in place of the hero. He was now a male hero seeking recognition, status, and personal legend. His inflated male ego needed retaliation and revenge. He was no longer in pursuit of justice without ego motives. He had now become a vigilante, seeking justice his way by whatever means, with all the contamination of political ego motives possible. In the manner of the old west, the responsible ones would be brought in dead or alive meaning, primarily, Saddam Hussein. What the world was supposed to accept as a Lone Ranger in pursuit of legitimate justice really became an expression of our country's unconscious complexes of fear, anger, and retaliation unleashed in an emotional explosion rather than through the logic that uncontaminated justice brings to action.

The second story, though seemingly different from the heroic motif of the Lone Ranger, is reflected in the historic figure still held in the hearts and collective memory of the Muslim world known as Salahadin or Saladin. He was born into a prominent Kurdish family in 1137/38 in Tikrit, Mesopotamia. On the very night of his birth, his father Najm ad-Din Ayyub, fled with his family from danger to Aleppo and entered into the service of Imad ad-Din Zangi ibn Aq Sonqur, the Turkish governor in Northern Syria. Salahadin grew up in Ba'lbek and Damascus, showing more interest in religious studies than military training and adventures. Yet, it was the latter that eventually earned him the name of "Salahadin the Victorious." This change to a military focus began when he joined the staff of his uncle Asad ad-Din Shirkuh, a top ranking military commander under the amir Nureddin, son and successor of Zangi. Through family connections and innate talent, he quickly rose to power after three successful military campaigns led by Shirkuh into Egypt to prevent territory established from the first crusade from falling back into Latin-Christian hands.

After Shirkuh's death, Saladin, in 1169, at the age of 31 was appointed commander of the Syrian troops and vizier of Egypt, becoming its sole ruler and, later still, uniting under his own leadership all the Muslim territories of Syria, Northern Mesopotamia, Palestine, and Egypt. This rise in military power required political maneuvering, timely deaths, and calculated military genius. Though he remained faithful to the Syrian military commander, Nureddin, that relationship ended with the latter's death in 1174. Egypt provided Saladin the financial base to raise a well-disciplined army which he led into Syria to claim the regency on behalf of the young son of his former suzerain. His interest, however, was not to be the head of a country but to unite all of Islam under one banner in order to be the military force required to recapture Jerusalem from the Latin Christians who had taken it 88 years prior.

It must be pointed out that Islam, like medieval Christianity, was not united. Divisions were everywhere established along political, national, and religious lines in both worlds. In that sense, Salahadin, like Richard I of England, as we will later see, had the politically difficult task of wining and dining, sometimes with tooth and dagger, the opposing forces in his own territory. The paradox of his need to unify Islam was his regretful need to spill Muslim blood, sometimes with the aid of Christian allies. It was no different for the European leaders. Each had to convince by word or sword the historical enemies in their own backyard to lay their old grievances aside and unite for the sake of a cause greater than their local skirmishes. Each successfully did this but with great difficulty and for a limited period on both sides.

Salahadin was a great leader who inspired his followers to take up arms and follow him on what was his single most personal directive that motivated his career: to stay devoted to the idea of "*Jihad*" (holy war), the Muslim equivalent to the Christian idea of crusade.

> He had chosen the paths of holy war and had equipped himself with the weapons of *Jihad*, unquestioning obedience and fanatical hatred of all that opposed the faith. It was these weapons that he must unleash against the remaining men who had stayed loyal to Nur-al-Din, a great Muslim like himself but now merely a memory. Saladin's hatred of spilling Muslim blood did not affect his zealots, who fought in the front line and sought martyrdom on the blade not of the infidels but of their own coreligionist.[26]

---

26 Geoffrey Regan, *Lionhearts, Richard I, Saladin and the Era of the Third Crusade* (New York: Walker & Company, Inc., 1998), p. 53.

In the end, what wounded him more than any defeat under the sword of Richard I was the renewed divisiveness of his beloved Islam after he drove Richard I from the Holy Lands and his retaking of Jerusalem.

What endeared him in Muslim history, however, was not this rise to power, but what he did with it. Like the Lone Ranger's resolve to bring justice to the West, Salahadin was resolved to bring his own understanding of justice in two important ways. The first was to rid the Muslim world of the dissension and intense rivalry that had divided it for so long and prevented it from being a unified power equal to the Christian Crusaders. He encouraged the growth of Muslim religious institutions, founded colleges and mosques, and worked to bring about moral regeneration which he inspired through personal example. His reputation grew as a generous and virtuous but firm ruler. He sought to recreate in his realm some of the same enthusiasm that proved valuable to the first generations of Muslims that enabled them to conquer half of the known world at that time.

The second event that signaled a return to the Muslim sense of justice occurred October 2, 1187, when the Franks surrendered Jerusalem after 88 years to the Sultan's army. In contrast to the blood spilled when the Christians had taken it, Salahadin ordered his army to treat the inhabitants in a civilized and courteous manner. This greatest of successes reduced the crusaders to the occupation of just three cities, the most important being Tyre, which became the rallying point for the call for a third crusade to recapture Jerusalem.

This defeat shocked the Western world, causing Pope Gregory VIII to order the third crusade to regain the Holy City. This summons to battle united conflicting medieval kingdoms under one cause that enlisted men all the way from the peasantry to the nobility along with famous knights and the leaders of three countries. From England came Richard the Lion Hearted; from France King Philip II; and from Germany came Emperor Frederick Barbarossa. These were the three most important men in Western Europe, showing just how important this mission was.

Emperor Frederick drowned on his way, which weakened his army, leaving only a handful that continued to the Middle East. Later King Philip II, being exhausted from a long but successful siege of the port of Acre, left for France. That left only one of the Western leaders finally making it to the outskirts of Jerusalem, Richard I. By this point, his army was exhausted and Richard himself was sick with a fever. In a strange request, he appealed to Salahadin, his enemy, for fresh water and fresh fruit. Salahadin met this request both because his Muslim faith required that he meet the request of the needy and quite possibly, also, to spy on Richard's army. The Muslim army realized that by this stage of the long conflict, Richard the Lion Hearted had only 2000 good soldiers and 50 knights to use in battle, which was hardly large enough to take Jerusalem. The result was a truce between them known as the Peace of Ramla that allowed pilgrims from the West to visit Jerusalem without being harassed, though Jerusalem would remain in Muslim control. Additionally, the whole coast was to be in Christian hands.

Though Richard I and Salahadin were fierce warriors who accompanied their own men into battle, each was known also for his generosity and military chivalry. Once when Richard was wounded, Salahadin offered the services of his personal physician, which was no small matter since Islamic medical practice, then, was considered far superior to Western medicine. Again, when Richard lost his horse at Arsuf, Salahadin sent him two replacements. There was even a plan by Richard to have his sister marry Salahadin's brother though she refused because, as a

Christian, she did not want to marry a Muslim. As for Richard, he personally forgave the man who shot him with an arrow and ordered his men to spare his life just before he died—an order they disregarded after their leader died.

As for Salahadin, most of what he had accomplished began to slip away shortly after Richard left the Holy Lands. After many long years of battle under sometimes unbearable conditions, he died in 1193 at Damascus. This was only one year after the peace agreement with Richard that ended the third crusade. Because of his generosity to those in need, there was not even enough money left to pay for his funeral.

In the end, the Western crusade proved little. Richard never returned to the Holy Lands and, at the age of forty-three, met an untimely death by an arrow during what historians believe was an unnecessary battle. By contrast, Salahadin grew to be respected in both the Muslim and Western worlds and reestablished the foundation of Muslim justice and self-respect, though as future history would prove, these would again be eroded. Yet, for even a short time, by retaking Jerusalem, he restored pride and self-respect to the Muslim community.

To return Jerusalem to Muslim control was to restore one of the most sacred sites to the greater *umma* community. Here was an outer symbol of the collective Self bringing together not only a unification of the Islamic people but also the feminine and masculine sides of life. In other words, the masculine side of this is to see that Jerusalem was the central seat of power and domination in that part of the world and to militarily bring it back under Muslim control. The feminine side of this was experienced in the unification of the people as well as the recapture of Jerusalem which symbolized the soul of the Islam. Through the personage of Salahadin, the collective ideal of the Muslim hero dedicated to justice for justice sake in the fullest sense of that word was reestablished. The veil of ignorance and distortion was lifted at least for a short while to reveal the deeper and more humane understanding of the *Qur'an*.

Though both the Lone Ranger and Salahadin represent mythic importance for their respective cultures in the pursuit of humane justice, they eventually came to be used by the political powers, rallying cry for motives far less ideal and reflected in wars and terrorist acts that have caused death and suffering to untold numbers of people.

THE MAKING OF HISTORY

No one can claim to be immune to the spirit of his own epoch
or to possess anything like a complete knowledge of it.[27]

Salahadin had liberated the Holy City of Jerusalem, a sacred city to Jews, Christians, and Muslims alike. Jerusalem is the symbol of promise and transcendence. Salahadin restored Muslim control of Jerusalem and defeated the European threat against Islam. The recapturing of Jerusalem restored to the Islamic community a sense of wholeness, constellating the Self. The archetypal energy of Salahadin, symbol of the Self, restored a sense of power of the Muslim people.

In 1929, in response to the Balfour Declaration declaring British support for a Jewish homeland in Palestine, Al-Sha'ir Al-Qarawi wrote the following poem:

> Saladin! Your people are calling upon you to rise from the dead; your chivalry would not allow you to sleep while they are on the alert.
>
> The crusaders have forgotten the lesson they received at your hands, so come back and remind them.[28]

---

27 C.G. Jung, CW 13 ¶ 153.

28 Khalid Sulaiman, *Palestine and Modern Arab Poetry* (London: Zed Books Ltd., 1984), p. 59.

The spirit of Salahadin as redeemer and savior still lives within the psyche of the Islamic world. But what is it that Salahadin has defended and restored? The Islamic world since Salahadin lived in isolation until the middle of the nineteenth century when Europe began diplomatic relationships with the Middle East. The Western world has had little exposure to Islamic culture and people, thereby minimizing its understanding and knowledge of Islam. The world split into separate parts being both psychologically and physically dissociated from one another. Hardly any westerner knows the central unifying prayerful call—a call that contains the central creed that unites the entire Islamic *umma*.

To begin to understand the Islamic world, one needs to hear the Muezzins call recited five times a day bringing Muslims all over the world to prayer.

> God is the most Great! I testify that there is no god but God. I testify that Muhammad is the Messenger of God. Come to prayer! Come to Salvation! God is the most Great! There is no god but God.[29]

The voice of the call resounds bringing consciousness of God and His Messenger Muhammad.

Muhammad was born in 570 C.E. He was orphaned at the age of two and raised by his uncle in Mecca. At forty years of age, in the year 610 C.E., Muhammad had his first revelation from God. He consulted his wife Khadija who supported and encouraged Muhammad to share his revelations with the community. If it were not for Khadija, the feminine, the female, he may not have brought the word of God to the Arab people forming their own book called the *Qur'an* which means

---

29 Paul Lunde, *Islam* (London, New York, Munich, Melbourne, Delhi: DK Publishing, 2002), p. 19.

"recitation." Muhammad established Islam, meaning "submission," and brought the word of Allah to the Arab people. Those who converted to Islam were known as Muslims, meaning "one who submits." Muhammad was the messenger who brought the existing chaotic world to its knees in recognition of the greater Self, the whole, verses rivaling tribes. Islam became the final and perfect revelation from God superseding Judaism and Christianity which were the precursors to Islam. God's word was incomplete and corrupted by the people of the Book, but the benevolent and ever-merciful Allah gave the last warning through the words of the final prophet, Muhammad, the "seal of the prophets."

When Muhammad's uncle died, his life became threatened without the protection of his uncle's clan. The prophet and his followers then needed to leave Mecca to begin a new Islamic community in Medina in the year 622 C.E. This migration, the *hijra*, is the beginning of the Islamic calendar. Muhammad governed a new Islamic community through the revelations of God's laws. The Muslims fought and conquered surrounding tribes then returned to Mecca and defeated the established tribal elders by breaking the icons of the old pagan gods thus reclaiming the *Ka'ba* and establishing it as the center of the universe. Muhammad's victories over neighboring tribes laid the foundation of the Islamic community.

Islam is based on five pillars. The first and most important is that there is only one God, Allah, and Muhammad is the final prophet. The *Shehada*, literally meaning "profession of faith" manifests as: "I testify there is no god but God and Muhammad is the messenger of God."[30] As in the prophetic religions preceding Islam, the most important message is the idea of one God versus surrounding tribes practicing worship of many gods;

---

30 Lunde, *Islam*, p. 19.

monotheism versus polytheism. For Muslims, the message is delivered by Muhammad as the final word. Second: A Muslim prays to God five times a day. Third: A Muslim fasts the month of Ramadan. Fourth: A Muslim makes a pilgrimage to Mecca if possible. Pillars two, three and four give structure to keeping conscious the importance of one's relationship to God and a space for that relationship. Fifth: A Muslim gives alms to the poor. From a Jungian point of view, a Muslim needs to pay homage to the inferior parts of the collective soul. In giving support to those disenfranchised people, a Muslim projects his/her own disenfranchised parts. Homage is paid to the poor, the sick and undeveloped parts of the giver's psyche.

Sometimes considered the Sixth pillar is the idea of *Jihad*. *Jihad* means "struggle." The greater *Jihad* is the inner struggle within each individual against evil and the surrender to God. The lesser *Jihad* is the struggle against the enemies of Islam protecting it through holy war. Paralleling this is Jung's suggestion that the inner psychological struggle of integrating the darkness into the light, unconscious into consciousness, is the moral path. As Jung stated,

> Neurosis is self-division. In most people the cause of the division is that the conscious mind wants to hang on to its moral ideal, while the unconscious strives after its unmoral ideal which the conscious mind tries to deny. Men of this type want to be more respectable than they really are. But the conflict can easily be the other way about. Extremes should therefore be avoided as far as possible, because they always arouse suspicion of their opposite.[31]

The moral path, then, according to Jung, would be to struggle, the *Jihad*, into awareness the split off unmoral part

---

31 C.G. Jung, *Two Essays on Analytical Psychology*, CW 7 (New York: Pantheon Books, 1953), ¶ 18.

forging a middle path which incorporates the knowledge of the unmoral and the standard of the moral ideal.

Muhammad died in 632 C.E. He had accomplished the task of unifying disparate ethnic elements and cultures together. He created an Islamic community, *umma*, transcending nation, tribe or clan, where all members of the faith are considered equal in the eyes of God. The *Qur'an* spelled out the codes of behavior and laws Muslims were to live by. The *Sunnah*, meaning "precedent," is a compilation of the behaviors of the prophet remembered by the relatives and friends who surrounded him. Muhammad represents the choice of a moral life, a life worth following. Within the *Sunnah*, the *Hadith* was written which included the traditions and reports of the sayings of Muhammad. The *Qur'an* and *Sunnah* are the physical manifestations left by Muhammad and inspired by the divine word. They are the foundation and blueprint of Islam.

Extrapolated from the *Qur'an*, *Sunnah*, and *Hadith* (analogies and consensus of the community) leading scholars and jurists devised a uniform legal system called *Sharia*. The *Sharia* is considered sacred law instructed by God that includes rules regarding worship, ritual, conduct, and legal contracts i.e. commercial, marriage, divorce, and inheritance. Interpretation of *Sharia* was closed in the tenth century, resulting in the continuance of the same practices today.

Upon Muhammad's death, a successor was chosen to lead the Islamic community. Abu Bakr, Muhammad's closest friend and father of his favorite wife A`isha, became the first *Caliph*. He reunited the Muslims after the prophet's death and began the expansion of Islam outside Arabia. Umar was the second *Caliph* spreading Islam to Persia, Syria, Palestine, and Egypt. When Umar was assassinated, Uthman was chosen to succeed him. He expanded the empire to Libya and Armenia and began conflict with the Byzantines. After Uthman was killed, Ali was chosen as his replacement. The first four Caliphs are known as the Rightly-Guided Caliphs because they all had heard the revelations from the prophet himself and been guided by his example.

After Ali, the split in Islam began between the *Shi's* and *Sunni* Muslims. The *Shi's* believed that the *Caliph* needed to be related to Muhammad by blood and therefore did not recognize the Caliphs after the first four. This difference created hostility and conflict between the two groups. This situation became the external reflection of the collective psyches inner struggle of one-sidedness that did not consider its opposite thus creating a division and conflict which would threaten the whole and all its parts. This conflict between the *Shi* and *Sunni* continues today causing wars within and between Islamic countries.

The fifth *Caliph* of the Umayyad dynasty was the governor of Syria who moved the capital from Medina to Damascus. By 749 C.E. with the emergence of the Abbasid dynasty in Persia, Baghdad, meaning "gift from God," became the capital of the *caliphate* and the wealthiest city in the world rivaled only by Constantinople. It later collapsed in 1258 C.E. when conquered by the Mongols. The Islamic borders continued to widen in 685 C.E. bringing Islam to the borders of China. The Berbers conquered Spain in 713 C.E. and, from the Atlantic, Islam expanded eastward to India.

Simultaneously, the Umayyads created a dynasty in Andalusia from the middle of the eighth century to the beginning of the tenth century. The great cities of this area, Cordova, Granada and Toledo, became the most urbane and richest cities in Europe. The *Caliphate* of Al-Andalus supported intellectual and scientific exploration from Jews, Christians, and Muslims all living together. This sophisticated empire contributed ideas and technologies throughout the world, known today for its massive libraries and translations of Greek manuscripts.

As Al-Andalus began to collapse, the Fatimids of Egypt gained power. Cairo was built and became the wealthiest city in the world in the eleventh century rivaling the power of the *Caliphate* of the Abbasids. In the thirteenth century, Genghis Khan entered the borders of the Islamic world toppling the Abbasids and expanding to Iran on the east and Anatolia on the west. The Mongol dynasty ruled the Islamic territories until 1380. Most of the Mongols who remained embraced Islam.

The next dynasty to rise shifted the focus of Islam to Anatolia (Turkey) resulting in the rise of the Ottoman Empire. With the conquest of Constantinople in 1453 C.E., a new *Caliphate* was set up, and in 1529 C.E., Sulayman the Magnificent made the Ottomans a world power. The empire included Northern Africa encompassing Algiers, Tunis, Tripoli, Egypt, and Ethiopia, the Middle East including western Arabia, Palestine, Syria, Mesopotamia, Georgia, and Iraq, as well as, Southern Russia and the European countries of Anatolia, Greece, and Hungary. The end of Ottoman invincibility and the beginning of Western control in the Middle East occurred with the invasion of Egypt by Napoleon in 1798 C.E. By the mid nineteenth century, England and France allied with the Ottomans against the Russians in the Crimean war. The "eastern question" addressed which of the great powers would get the provinces of the weakening Ottoman Empire. This question preoccupied European politics for the rest of the nineteenth century and was a contributory cause of WWI. By 1914 C.E., the Ottomans sealed their fate with their alliance with Germany, causing the downfall of the bankrupt empire.

Simultaneous to the Ottoman Empire was the successful Safavid dynasty in Persia from 1500–1722 C.E. and the Mughal dynasty in India from 1526–1738 C.E. Both dynasties were powerful and added a different dimension to the Islamic world.

This historical review brings us to modern world politics and the concerns of the Islamic world today. As indicated above, the Islamic world enjoyed the existence of powerful and rich civilizations filled with accomplishment and pride. Psychiatrist and Jungian Analyst, Hechmi Dhaoui, analyzes the difficulties of the present psychological situation in the Islamic world as directly related to their glorified and triumphant past. As Dhaoui writes in response to 9/11 in his chapter "From Wahhabism to Talibanism," "hopefully, Arab Muslims will creatively adjust to our current epoch and abandon self destructive nostalgia for an idealized past."[32] The twentieth century, however, changed the Islamic world from self-rule to colonization and exploitation. The collective ego identity of the Islamic world felt powerless and inferior to the dynasties of the past.

At the end of WWI, the League of Nations divided the Ottoman Empire and distributed its parts to Russia, France, and England. The colonial period transformed the Islamic world even among countries not part of the mandate, protectorate, or colonies. Muslims began building resentment toward European superiority. By the end of WWII, all Arabic countries gained independence from colonial powers, but the advances attained by the West technologically and scientifically clearly left the Islamic societies feeling left behind. Islamic nations began importing Western ideas and customs, seeing them as superior and more evolved while, paradoxically, a backlash resisting Western infiltration emerged fighting to keep traditional customs and values intact.

---

32 Luigi Zoja and Donald Williams, editors, *Jungian Reflections of September 11*, Hechmi Dhaoui, "From Wahhabism to Talibanism" (Einsiedeln, Switzerland: Daimon Verlag, 2002.

The establishment of the state of Israel in 1948 C.E. as promised by the British in the Balfour Declarations created a homeland for the Jewish people. Ninety-two percent of the population was Muslim or Christian Arabs. Three quarters of a million Palestinians were displaced from their homes and moved to refuge camps, which later added more residents due to subsequent wars in 1956, 1967, and 1973. Muslims throughout the Middle East now regard American support for Israel as indifference to the plight of the Palestinians and as an attack on Islam and further colonization of the region.

In 1951 Muhammad Musadek overthrew the Shah of Iran to establish a democracy and become the first prime minister. He represented anti-colonialism and nationalized the oil, keeping the profits of Iranian oil production in Iran, thereby increasing the profits from sixteen percent under the Shah to one hundred percent. In 1953 the democracy was overthrown by a coup, called "Operation AJAX," that was incited and supported by the British government and the CIA. The son of the previous shah, Shah Reza, was installed, returning fifty percent of the oil to world companies. The Islamic Revolution in 1979 overthrew Shah Reza and reinstated an Islamic theocracy controlled by *Sharia* and religious clerics. Ayatollah Khomeini became an inspiration for the Islamic world, defending Islam against "the Great Satan," (America) and influencing the expansion of Islamic movements. The Islamic cultural ego, having been beaten down by decades of Western exploitation, now projected onto the Western culture their own unresolved shadow issues. The First Gulf War and sanctions against Iraq following the war reinforced the power of American force and its impact on the Middle East. American troops left on Saudi soil, the sacred territory of Islam, felt like an occupation and intrusion in the Muslim soul and soil.

Twenty-three percent of the world population is Muslim according to a 2009 demographic study. Islam is the world's second largest religion after Christianity. Islam is the predominant religion in the Middle East, in Africa, and in some parts of Asia. Approximately fifty countries are Muslim majorities. The collapse of the Soviet Union liberated the practice of religion, giving voice to Islam in Kazakhstan, Tajikistan, Uzbekistan, Kyrgyzstan, and Turkmenistan as Afghanistan imposed extreme Muslim behavioral laws. Islam today is spreading throughout Africa, establishing itself north of the Sahara desert, Egypt, and Nigeria having the most populace Muslim communities and gaining influence and power in Southern countries. Presently, the Sudanese government has imposed genocide on Sudanese natives unwilling to convert to Islam. Around sixty-two percent of Muslims live in Asia. Indonesia, with the exception of Bali, is the largest Muslim country by population home to 12.9% of the world's Muslims. About twenty percent live in Arab countries. In the Middle East, the non-Arab countries of Turkey and Iran are the largest Muslim majority countries. Other parts of the world host large immigrant Muslim communities; in Western Europe, for instance, Islam is the second largest religion after Christianity though it represents less than five percent of the total population. In the United States, Islam is the fastest growing religion. According to the Council on American-Islamic Relations in 2011, seven million Americans are Muslim which represent 2.2% of the United States population. The rate of increased Muslim population and its continued rise and exponential growth gives Islam a serious place on the world stage that the Western world needs to acknowledge and respect. The Western world cannot continue to deny or devalue the presence of a substantially significant Islamic population. The greater share of the West, however, apparently chooses to live within a narrow definition of the Islamic world, limiting vital knowledge and perceptions for the sake of creating a black and white view of the other.

Educating the West is an attempt to lift the veil of ignorance regarding the Islamic world in the hope of taking back the projections. Muslim countries have concerns with American interest in the Islamic world. Many believe that America is exploitive with interests of economic gain and is an enemy of Islam while oppressing the poor. Since the end of the colonialization by Europe, Muslims have seen America support the deportation of Palestinians, incite the overthrow of an Iranian democracy, and invade Iraq with no apparent motive. Americans are seen as self-serving with the power of a bully.

Current anti-American and anti-Western attitudes are not new to the Islamic world. Sayyid Qutb, an Egyptian philosopher of the fifties and sixties, wrote a manifesto for the terrorist wing of fundamentalist Islamic organizations. Qutb wrote *In the Shade of the Koran*, which is a voluminous work drawn from the study of the *Qur'an*. Qutb believed that the crusaders and Zionists have been conspiring for centuries to destroy Islam. He wanted to turn Islam into a political movement to create a new society based on *Qur'anic* principles. He pictured a resurrected *Caliphate* and Islamic nations governed by a theocracy strictly enforcing *Sharia*. He believed that social problems of alcoholism, drug addiction, loss of morality, and man's basic unhappiness was due to placing faith in the power of human reason, which, he said, created a "tyranny of technology over life." The source of man's dysfunction resides in the theology of Judaism and Christianity. Judaism, according to Qutb, has become rigid and lifeless while Christianity dilutes and perverts the message of Jesus. Christianity promotes the idea of Jesus as the messiah versus Islam's belief in Jesus as a prophet. In addition, Qutb believes Christianity's fatal flaw is in rejecting important Jewish tenants as well as separating the secular and the sacred. "Render unto Caesar what is Caesars and unto God what is God's" (Matthew 22:21) splits the physical and spiritual world. The modern world with liberal ideas brings confusion and a lack of spiritual direction. Ideas of democracy separate from a religious theocracy threaten the Islamic vision of a community where government and religion both rule. Qutb's work is anti-Semitic describing Jews as hateful, diabolical with never ending conspiracies against Muhammad and Islam. His attitude regarding freedom for women allies with the restrictiveness of the authority of God versus other sources of authority such as secular government. His recommended course of action was a revolutionary program that would relieve the psychological pressure of modern life and connect man with God.

Qutb was hanged in 1966 after ten years in prison because he was perceived by Nasser as a threat to pan-Arabism. Qutb was a member of the Muslim Brotherhood, Egypt's Islamist movement. His philosophies are the blueprint of most of today's Islamist organizations ranging from a moderate interpretation of his philosophies to the most extreme interpretation as embodied by Al Qaeda. Qutb expressed one side of the tension in the polarity of secular versus theocratic. While embracing the scientific advances of modernism, he challenged modernity in favor of traditionalism.

Ideas and attitudes expressed by Qutb had a breeding ground in Afghanistan where varied factions and strange bedfellows allied with one another to overcome and defeat the Soviet invasion. Muslims from other countries came to Afghanistan to join forces with the *mujahedin* and established an army that was supported by the United States in an effort to combat the spread of communism. The socially conservative countries of Pakistan and Saudi Arabia also supported this venture. Pakistan wanted a closer alliance with the United States because of the threat of

India on its border while Saudi Arabia had an opportunity to spread Islamic fundamentalism, *Wahabi* style, which was both anti-Iran and anti-*Shiite*. The common denominator for both countries was to solidify *Sunni* Islam to the area and thus expand its limits beyond the borders of Pakistan which was established for the sole purpose of creating a *Sunni* Muslim state. The Soviet Union collapsed in 1989. Islamic factions fought for dominance in the region while American interest in the area could have been summed up as benign neglect.

Jihadists who flocked to Afghanistan are now called "Afghans" no matter their country of origin and have now been taught to fight for an Islamic way of life. They are opponents of American and Israeli ideology and feel they have to protect the *umma* or Muslim world from American expansionism, which is viewed as an infection and psychologically understood as a cultural shadow dynamic. Al Qaeda was formed from the *Jihad* warriors who were initially from Pakistan, Saudi Arabia, Egypt, and Algeria. Many of these militants then took their brand of Islamist ideology back to their countries after the war and remained connected with the Al Qaeda network and/or established more radical splinter groups. At the same time, in 1990, the loosely defined Al Qaeda network chose Osama Bin Laden as their leader with the support of Pakistan and Saudi Arabia. Al Qaeda became pro-*Taliban* while Bin Laden became openly anti-American in 1991 during the Gulf War and U.S. support in Somalia. It took Washington until 1998 to identify Osama Bin Laden as enemy number one.

The first generation of Al Qaeda recruited the second generation who were volunteers without nationalistic loyalties. They were willing to fight from *Jihad* to *Jihad* no matter where in the world that may be. Most of these recruits are living in the West today on the margins of Western society as radical

Islamists dedicated to international terrorism.[33] Encouraged in national debates and international conflicts, Islamic organizations grew in number, influence and strength and, accordingly, need to join the dialogue with international leaders. The energy created by Islamic organizations throughout the world adds another variable to today's political instability, fueling the polarization in today's East–West conflict and creating the possibility of worldwide destruction.

A basic psychological premise here is that the more the ego refuses to be aware of the threat of unconscious material, what we do not know, the more threatening the complex is to the ego. Translated from an individual psychology to a relevant cultural psychology, the West, America in particular, remains ignorant and narrowly focused on Western attitudes toward Islam. The attitude of non-acceptance of Islamic culture creates a belief system fostering skewed perceptions of the "other." The lack of awareness of one's cultural projections that leads to unconscious behaviors fuels the threat of extremist Islamist terrorism, which focuses on American annihilation. Americans need to know the history of Islam and Islamic nationhood as well as their own history. *Jihadist, in reverse*, need to understand the history and culture of the West. Then each side, in pulling back their projections, can explore what messages are being sent and how that may be perceived by the "other." Without an understanding of the "other," it is easy to demonize and remain ignorant.

With modernity comes globalization which is not only a major threat to traditional Islam but also another highway for communicating Islamic thought and international terrorism. In a time of mass transportation and communication, the world has access to diverse and oppositional ideas. Computers have made

33 Oliver Roy, *Globalized Islam* (New York: Columbia University Press, 2004), p. 303.

available ideas that add new information to a one-sided dialogue, altering the ability of one perspective to dominate unchallenged. Globalization reduced the isolation felt by developing countries, opened international trade, and created new jobs. Internet access also connected anti-globalization activists creating a capacity to express their position and contact one another worldwide. Western lifestyles have influenced young Muslims through education, travel, computers, and cinema. Materialism inspires the desire for a secular society with up-to-date technology and scientific achievement. The new world of technology challenges the old ways as well as enhancing the emerging countries on the world scene economically.

Globalization rests on economic policies and practices. Joseph Stiglitz, winner of the 2001 Nobel Prize in economics, states that there are three main institutions that govern globalization and the third world's ability to achieve economic success. These are the IMF (the International Monetary Fund), the World Bank, and the WTO (World Trade Organization). The IMF was created to ensure global economic stability in response to the Great Depression. The World Bank was created to eradicate poverty by implementing economic strategies providing loans to poor countries. The WTO encourages free flow of goods throughout the world. These institutions have expanded their original mandates since the end of colonialism and the fall of communism, becoming dominant forces in the world economy. All countries needing help must comply with WTO policies and restrictions. Countries that want to participate in global markets must comply with market ideologies and theories. Participation requires countries to accept U.S. style capitalism as the only path to progress.[34]

---

34 Joseph Stiglitz, *Globalization and Its Discontents* (London: W.W. Norton Company Ltd., 2003) pp. 21-22.

The IMF, World Bank, and WTO are public institutions on a global level. The members selected to be finance ministers of each institution are connected to investment firms and banks throughout the financial community. The only country that has a veto is the United States thereby having more economic power than other participating countries. The West drives the globalization agenda which can be perceived as receiving a disproportionate share of benefits at the expense of developing countries. Policies imposed on countries that borrow money from the World Bank have to agree to engage in cutting deficits, raising taxes, or raising interest rates. The World Bank and IMF (the institution that gives final approval for any loan) become a permanent part of life with most developing countries. The IMF has access and control of government budgets, financial institutions, labor markets, how they spend money, and conduct trade policies thus creating an unbalanced advantage to Western economies over developing economies.[35]

The IMF has also insisted on maintaining tight monetary policies that lead to high interest rates that are another contributory factor to the impossibility of job creation. The IMF enforcement of capital market liberalization opens markets to an influx of what is called "hot money" into and out of the country leaving havoc and instability. Imposed "property rights" keep countries from producing their own products such as drugs, making it impossible to pay the higher prices for imported drugs. An example of this problem was a poor country's inability to afford AIDS drugs from the Western market leaving people to die. The IMF finally backed down in 2001 lowering international drug costs.[36]

---

35 Stiglitz, pp. 21-22.
36 Stiglitz, pp. 21-22.

challenger in jobs

The World Bank and IMF have failed in their mission. Despite promises of poverty reduction, poverty increased the last decade of the twentieth century by one hundred million people. In addition, both agencies have failed to ensure international economic stability. Joseph Stiglitz states,

> We have a system which might be called global governance without global government, one in which a few institutions, WB, IMF, and WTO, and a few players, the finance commerce and trade ministers, closely linked to certain financial and commercial interests, dominate the scene, but in which many of those affected by their decisions are left voiceless.[37]

People of developing countries wanting to compete for the global economic arena feel left behind and see the West as conspiring to keep it that way. Western financial institutions and the U.S. in particular hold the purse strings and the power to create or destroy countries economically. This breeds frustration and hatred and nurtures the negative projections of imperialism and exploitation onto the West, supporting the Islamist viewpoint of anti-globalization. These perceptions from the East lie behind the veil in the West, not seen or understood. Many Americans share the assumption that our economic values are good, inevitable, just, democratic, and worth sharing with the world. They believe that spreading these values will make the world become a healthier, safer, and peaceful collective. Feeling sure and righteous, the West ignores the perceptions of Islamic community labeling them as extremist or primitive.

Over the last few centuries, Western culture has seen a shift from *ethos*, from the belief in a divinely ordered *cosmos*, to *logos* or a faith in rational thought and practical action. Another consideration of what might be living under the veil of

---

37 Stiglitz, pp. 21-22.

consciousness is the meaning in the rise of fundamentalism. Historically fundamentalism has been a cosmic war between the forces of good and evil such as the Crusades. It has been a response to a painful transition to modernity. Fear and anxiety lie at the foundation of fundamentalist thought. It is a frantic desire to fill a void with certainty, to control the uncontrollable. Fear and rage against possible annihilation fosters the rigidity of belief that ancient dogma will conquer evil, restore God in the world, and change the world before it changes them.

Jung writes in *Symbols of Transformation* about the consequences of the shift from *mythos* to *logos* and states:

> The world had not only been deprived of its gods, but had lost its soul. Through the shifting of interest from the inner to the outer world, our knowledge of nature was increased a thousand fold in comparison to earlier ages, but knowledge and experience of the inner world were correspondingly reduced.[38]

While this transition is certainly not universal, it has contributed to a culture where materialism has prevailed. In this world, people who feel disenfranchised may turn to fundamentalism as a sanctuary from the pressures of modernity. Fundamentalism offers truth and stability to those who experience fear, anxiety, depression, and rage. It is a frantic desire to fill a void with certainty, to control the uncontrollable. Fear and rage against possible annihilation fosters fragility of belief that ancient dogma will conquer evil, restore God in the world, and change the world before it changes them.

An emptiness, a sense of meaninglessness has become a part of the modern experience, leading Nietzsche to claim that, "God is dead" and creates a craving for something more. The

---

38 C.G. Jung, *Symbols of Transformation*, CW 5, (Princeton, N.J.: Princeton University Press, 1956), ¶ 113.

forces of fundamentalism were waiting for its day which has approached with the ending of the second millennium. The power of fanatic Zionists, fundamentalist Christians, and extremist Muslims are a response to powerlessness and deprivation. Fundamentalism attempts to restore *mythos* by concretizing myth into literalism. Reclaiming the Old Testament, following the journey of Christ to the letter of the New Testament, and the literal interpretation of the *Koran* bring fundamentalists back to a time when God was in control fulfilling His promise to His people. Fundamentalist Christianity in the West collides with extreme Islam in the East in their lack of understanding of the "other," and claims certainty that their way is right and the way of God. Islamists have promised to restore the olden days of prosperity by restoring Islam to its purist roots. In some areas, religion has been hijacked to facilitate political agendas and further incite conflict. America is torn between fundamentalism and secular belief, and that conflict is mirrored within the Islamic world. The tension between traditional and modern is felt within each nation and reverberates around the world. This is again an example of the cultural ego feeling threatened by the unknown forces of the cultural unconscious. Unconscious feelings of inferiority, failure, loss of identity, and loss of self results in the ego reacting with literalism and certainty in life. Ideas of openness and exploration can balance anxiety of the unknown through self-reflection as well as encouraging internal and external dialogue.

A call to Salahadin is heard throughout the Islamic world. As modernism threatens traditionalism, democracy challenges theocracy and secularism jeopardizes religion, a resistance in opposition to Western ideology has increased in the Islamic world creating liberators and martyrs as today's modern heroes. Salahadin has been reincarnated in Sayyid Qutb, Osama Bin Laden, Arafat, and those unknown martyrs of Al Qaeda,

Hezbollah, Hamas, *Jihad* Islamism, National Front, Muslim Brotherhood, etc. Out of the pain of humiliation, dependence, inferiority, and feelings of exploitation, fundamentalism and violence defies westernization with the purification of Islam and the elimination of practices not sanctioned by the *Qur'an* and *Sunnah* that will ultimately lead to triumph over the enemy.

SHEHERAZADE

REDEMPTRESS AND TELLER OF TALES

O Shahrazad, that was a noble and admirable story. ... you have told me some things which were strange, and many that were worthy of reflection. I have listened to you for a thousand nights and one night, and now my soul is changed and joyful, it beats with an appetite for life.

O father of Shahrazad, O begetter of benediction, Allah has raised up your daughter to be the salvation of my people. Repentance has come to me through her.[39]

Islamic fundamentalists have as their jihadist template, Salahadin, who re-conquered the sacred cultural and religious center, Jerusalem. By this victory, he eliminated the collective pain of humiliation Muslims had carried for nearly a century. Standing along side Salahadin, however, and strangely equal to him is another figure, mythic in character, less talked about, but deeply embedded in Middle Eastern literary culture, the person of Sheherazade. Salahadin was a military liberator who gave his life to reunite the Muslim community by establishing them once again in their sacred home, and, who went on to establish educational and religious centers to help his people remember what being a Muslim was really about.

---

39 *The Thousand Nights and One Night*, Vol. 4, page 531.

In the same way, Sheherazade was also a liberator but of a different kind. As will be seen, her task also was to regain the soul of her people. She would do this, however, not with sword and lance but with stories that awakened the king to his narrow sighted fundamentalists killing behavior. These stories reminded him of the cultural soul he had long forgotten. She also becomes a template for any culture that has lost its collective soul and then responds to that loss with defensive fundamentalist behavior. It is not uncommon for any nation, culture, or religious collective to lose track of its *raison d'être,* to forget its creation stories that reflect how and why it came into being. Sheherazade not only identifies a common and basic collective problem but shows a way back that can enable a culture to individuate into its own unique future.

With this template in mind, the attacks of September 11, 2001, entrenched itself deep in the minds of people throughout the world causing reactions as divergent and profound as soul numbing grief and anger, or exuberant displays of joy and victory. For those who live on North American soil, this event and the international reaction became a marker of just how vulnerable we were, how interconnected we have always been to the politics of countries we hardly knew existed or could pronounce (Turkmenistan, Kyrgyzstan, Uzbekistan, Tajikistan, Kazakhstan, etc.). It showed us how worldwide sympathy for what we experienced could quickly turn to antagonism and disgust for the way we responded. It marked a rise in prejudice and harsh reaction against Muslim communities, grouping them together as having one intention, namely, to eliminate any who did not follow the prophet Muhammad.

For others, these events challenged us to face what we did not know and to come to terms with our lack of understanding about the historical events that set the collective psychological ground for such a violent act to occur. Because the Western world has been dominated by the Judeo/Christian view of life, few people except Muslims or scholars of religion have known much about Islam. Fortunately, now with little effort, anyone can have access to a plethora of information and documentaries on the richness of the Islamic religion and the people who honor it as the prophet, Muhammad, intended. Words that were once strange to us like *Shiite, Sunni, Taliban, hajj, Jihad, mullah, mujahideen,* and even *Koran* and Muhammad are now commonly referenced on talk radio, television, newspapers and magazines, and in private conversations.

What is not heard of and seems so important to a deeper understanding of the rich historical roots of Islam itself is any reference to that literary treasure most westerners have come to know as *The Thousand and One Nights* or more accurately *The Thousand Nights and One Night.*[40] We have heard Disney versions of Jinni's and Sultans, Ali Baba and the Forty Thieves, Aladdin's lamp and, maybe, Sheherazade. Yet, it is strange that no mention is made of this literary masterpiece at this time, for here we have story upon story of intrigue, humor, redemption, betrayal, forgiveness, being lost, being found, explosive anger, explosive joy, time warps, cliff hangers, and dramas one leading into the other for one thousand and one times making in the end one fantastic story. What is most important, however, is that this one grand story told in one thousand and one evolving steps has behind it a greater drama that, if understood, can act as a template for a deeper understanding of not only the world of Islam but also of our own.

---

40 The reader is referred to *The Thousand and One Nights: Commonly Called, in England, The Arabian Nights' Entertainments,* Ed. Edward Stanley Poole, Trans. by Edward William Lane, Publisher Chatto and Windus, 1839 – available from http://www.books.google.com as a free ebook. See also Mathers, Powys. *The Thousand Nights and One Night.* 4 Volumes, St. Martin's Press, (New York, 1972).

This is the story of Sheherazade, the teller of the thousand and one tales that, in the end, wrought the redemption she sought. In short paraphrased form,[41] this is the story that initiated the awesome task that Sheherazade willingly and dangerously undertook:

  There was once a king who had two sons, one tall named Shahryar and one small named Shahzaman. These brothers became kings after their father died and ruled justly in their own separate countries. It came to pass that Shahryar longed to visit his brother and sent his wazir to depart and invite his brother to come and visit. King Shahzaman accepted the invitation, made preparations and promptly departed. During the night, he remembered something he had forgotten and returned to his palace only to find that his wife was "stretched on her bed and being embraced by a black slave." In a rage he killed them both with his sword and continued on his journey. When he arrived at his brother's palace, he was seized by grief for what had happened but could not bear to tell his taller brother, King Shahryar. But then it happened one day that he saw that his own brother's wife with twenty of her slaves were in the garden when her husband was gone. A gigantic black slave entered and had sex with King Shahryar's wife. The slaves, in turn, all had their partners of their own the entire day. Reluctantly, King Shahzaman told his brother who verified this himself on another day when he had pretended to be gone.

Now that both the brothers experienced the same betrayal, they felt it better to depart from their kingdoms believing they had no right to royalty until

---

41 *The Thousand and One Nights: Commonly Called, in England, The Arabian Nights' Entertainments*, Ed. Edward Stanley Poole, Trans. by Edward William Lane, Publisher Chatto and Windus, 1839 – available from http://www.books.google.com as a free ebook.

they had found someone who had met a fate like theirs. They traveled far until they came to a tree in the middle of a lonely field near the salt sea. Shortly, they saw a column of black smoke that moved toward them. Terrified they climbed the tree. What they saw turned out to be a Jinni of great size carrying a box on his head. He put the box down and opened it revealing a beautiful woman, his wife. The Jinni, being tired, laid down and rested his head on his wife's knees and promptly fell asleep. Immediately, the woman freed herself from her husband and called to the two brothers to come down from the tree and have sex with her or she would threaten to awaken her husband who would kill them with the worst of deaths. The two kings were terrified to do so knowing this was no ordinary woman but eventually complied. Being pleased with their abilities, she took from a little bag a necklace of five hundred and seventy seal-rings which represented all the men who had coupled with her under her husband's nose. She demanded the two brothers to give her each one of theirs. Then she recounted her story that her husband had carried her off on the night of her marriage, imprisoned her in a coffer and placed it in a box and fastened it with seven chains then laid it at the bottom of the sea. "But he did not know that whenever any one of us women desires a thing, nothing can prevent her from it."

With these words, the brothers realized they had met someone who had suffered the same fate as they, the Jinni himself, and now felt ready to return to their homeland. When King Shahryar entered his palace, he cut his wife's head off along with all of the slaves, both men and women, and ordered his wazir to bring him a young virgin girl every night with whom he would have sex and then kill by morning. He did this for three years until there were very few young girls left. His own wazir had two daughters whom the wazir feared would be taken. They were beautiful and well-educated. The younger was Dunyazad and the older was Sheherazade. The latter especially "had read the books, the annals, and the legends of old kings, together with the histories of past peoples. She was known to possess knowledge of a thousand books of stories telling of the peoples, the kings, and the poets of bygone ages and of past time. She was sweetly eloquent of speech and to listen to her was music." It was arranged for her to marry King Shahryar with the possible fate of being killed herself or "be a ransom for the daughters of the Mussulmans and the cause of their deliverance out of the hands of the King." It was arranged that her younger sister would go with her into the king's bed chamber, sleep on the floor and, at a signal after the king had had sex with Sheherazade, would say. "Tell me, my sister, some of your stories of marvel that the night may pass pleasantly." Thus for one thousand and one nights, stories were told one evolving into the next that kept the king spell bound with curiosity and Sheherazade alive.

This opening places the "Thousand and One Nights" in the category of fairy tales as they are found throughout the world. Fairy tales carry important symbolic meaning for more deeply understanding the culture in which they evolved. Here will be found issues that are not addressed openly or consciously in the existing cultural attitudes but which will be carried by the unconscious world that are a part of the "personality" of every culture.

If an individual has an unlived or unconscious side that can show itself in unconscious ways, so does a culture. No individual or culture can be fully aware of itself. At the same time, a serious and reflective study of one's history provides a way of collectively learning what a culture wants or does not want to have happen again. To the extent that this is done, a culture, or any collective, grows in self-awareness. In the United States, for example, the long history of repression of racial and gender inequalities reached an awareness level in the twentieth century which could no longer be avoided. It is true that a history of violence and intensified resistance to these changing attitudes became the unfortunate prelude toward making real for the lives of millions of people the democratic ideals on which our country was founded. It is, also, true that continued advance of equal justice in just these two areas are still needed. Nevertheless, the greatest share of the North American culture knows what it does not want any longer.

As individuals, we are revealed to ourselves in the course of a lifetime, or, at least it is to our benefit if we do. So with a culture as it evolves over long periods of history. This "finding out," however, can often be painful, frightening, sometimes wonderfully enlightening but often destructive to the extent we do not take responsibility for ourselves but project the unlived world onto others be they individuals or nations. It is also true that individuals change more quickly than nations. The collective personality of any nation is huge and usually takes decades, and more often, centuries to change.

At present, what needs to change and the issues that need to be faced are often reflected in film, edgy literature, heretical ideas, governmental and ecclesiastical protest, as well as cultural symptoms such as extreme violence in our streets, addictive behavior, a rise in depression and anxiety, feelings of alienation, and a frenetic living pace that is de-souling America.

Long ago, however, these symptoms were seen in fairy-tale-like stories. One of the great researchers in fairy tales is the late Dr. Marie-Louise von Franz. In her book *Introduction to Fairy Tales*, she states:

> The fairy tale itself is its own best explanation; that is, its meaning is contained in the totality of its motifs connected by the thread of the story. The unconscious is, metaphorically speaking, in the same position as one who has had an original vision or experience and wishes to share it. Since it is an event that has never been conceptually formulated he is at a loss for means of expression. When a person is in that position, he makes several attempts to convey the thing and tries to evoke, by intuitive appeal and analogy to familiar material, some response in his listeners; and never tires of expounding his vision until he feels they have some sense of the content.[42]

This is the position and, in many ways, the description of Sheherazade. She has the "original vision or experience and wishes to share it." In fact, she knows intuitively that sharing it even with potential threat to her own life, is the only way to bring redemption to both the feminine and masculine principles. She does make "appeal and analogy to familiar material" and "never tires of expounding [her] vision until [she] feels they [in this case the King] have some sense of the content."

Again von Franz writes:

> I have come to the conclusion that all fairy tales endeavor to describe one and the same psychic fact, but a fact so complex and far-reaching and so difficult for us to realize in all its different aspects that hundreds of tales and thousands of repetitions with a musician's variations are needed until this unknown fact is delivered into consciousness. This unknown fact is what Jung calls the Self, which is the psychic totality of an individual and also, paradoxically, the regulating center of the collective

---

42 Marie-Louise von Franz, *The Interpretation of Fairy Tales* (New York: Spring Publications, 1970). p. 1.

unconscious. Every individual and every nation has its own modes of experiencing this psychic reality.[43]

This expresses the awesome task before Sheherazade, namely to describe the fundamental truth needing to be made conscious, but a truth "so complex and far-reaching" that it would take "hundreds of tales and thousands of repetitions" until the King is awakened to conscience and consciousness of those factors and attitudes that foster life and do not destroy it. It is that truth embodied in the notion of the Self that Sheherazade commissions herself to convey to the King and, via this transmission, to her entire culture.

The king archetypally represents the dominant structures of any culture known through its accepted ways of thinking politically and religiously, through its laws, rules of conduct, attitudes toward oneself and others, and the ways of doing business. When these structures break down, it is reflected in story form through the theme of a sick or dying king. Here is what is meant by the animus of which Carl Jung spoke but expressed in a cultural context.

In the same manner, when the king no longer has a queen, as in the story of Sheherazade, these so called kingly structural dominants are only that, namely, devoid of the Queen, or anima feminine energy, there is little to no feeling relationship toward what these structural dominants stand. The archetypal truth behind the queen symbolism is in the feeling/relational life a person and a people give to these dominants. She is the reason individuals live and die for their country with all its varied structured codified ways of looking at life. When the queen is absent, sick, or imprisoned, the cultural dominants are lifeless. There is no longer the spirit of the law, there is just the law. But,

---

43 Von Franz, pp. 1-2.

just as the king can, in a persona manner, appear to be the most humble of citizens, he can also be the most ruthless. Such a leader may appear at public gatherings in good congenial form, shaking the hands of elders and rubbing the heads of children, while enforcing the most brutal of policies toward any who would dissent against his government. Similarly, what the queen represents as an animating life force can be dedicated to the highest of ideals or to the most debased forms of behavior. In other words, it is possible that our views and beliefs can so animate our behavior, that we can do the most diabolical things in the name of religion, politics, or personal idiosyncrasies.

There are many themes surrounding the archetypal energies of king and queen. When both are functioning in service to the greater Self, the kingdom flourishes. When one or the other is missing or one is ruthless over the other, illness pervades the land, an illness that today can be felt as a cultural anxiety, malaise, and excessive violence. But herein lays the problem because the king might not only be devoid of a queen, he might have the wrong queen.

So it is with any extremist group be they political or religious. Today we know only too well the passion that drives extremists in Islam, Christianity, and Judaism and of their willingness to die "for the cause." The feminine that guides them is literally or psychologically an anima of death, dedicated to a limited worldview that negates anything not of their own soil. So, it is not only the structural form of life expressed through whatever philosophical, theoretical, or doctrinal views we hold that matters, but the nature of the feeling attitudes and commitments that foster them.

Without a king and queen dedicated to and in service to the Self, the people will despair. They will lose connection with the deeper meaning of life and settle for simplistic answers and a literalized religious life devoid of mystery and awareness of the deep inner truths that evolve in a culture. This is why Sheherazade is so important a figure in this ongoing story. She is the true queen, the one who remembers and is in service to life. It is said that she "had read the books, the annals, and the legends of old kings, together with the histories of past peoples. Also she was credited with possessing a thousand books of stories telling of the peoples, the kings, and the poets of bygone ages and of past time. She was sweetly eloquent of speech and to listen to her was music." In short form, she remembered and honored the soul of her people, its history, its ancestors, its poetry and music. It was this and only this that would save her and eventually the king himself.

But, let us be reminded of what started this drama. It was betrayal. The queen had sex with her black slave in the king's absence. Things get cloudy, however, when we consider what is one person's betrayal is another person's "so what." An innocent act or statement by one person can be seen as a betrayal by another. Betrayal by its very nature implies a relativity of moral perception and is always felt more powerfully by the one experiencing it. The one who has committed the act of betrayal often does not see it as betrayal if he or she can give sometimes convincing reasons for the behavior. In the case of the king's wife, her act, on the surface of things, does seem by traditional definition an act of clear betrayal. So be it at that level. But what would she say if she could speak for herself. One could imagine her describing what it was like to live in the confines of the palace walls, luxurious as they were. What was it like for her to be the king's wife rather than he the queen's husband?

Though her act can be seen as betrayal, it also can be viewed as an act of rebellion. Rebellion carries within its very nature a drive for freedom. Assuming that the queen was not bereft of any sense of morality, then, we are left with a rebellious reaction to an overly contained and confined woman. She could not have chosen a better way to rebel. She had sex with a black slave, the true opposite of her husband. Her lover was a black man, the unfortunate carrier of so many shadow projections of a culture that leans too far to the white. He was a slave, devoid of possessions, freedom, and the right to control his own life. Her husband was white, free, wealthy, and the one who controlled a kingdom.

This imaginative view of what the queen did is conceivable if we remember that the other brother was also a king and was also betrayed by his queen in the same manner. Two brothers, two queens. What is going on here? What is this reflecting about any culture where the theme of betrayal by woman is so emphasized? From a literary point of view, this doubling effect only serves to emphasize the pervasiveness of the problem affecting the kingdom. The heart of the drama that set in motion the thousand and one nights is contained in this betrayal of two queens and the dynamics that instigated their rebellion.

We have heard of the containment of women in the Islamic world. Today it is not the palatial walled gardens of the king but a *burca* and veil that keep her confined when politically imposed by extremist Islamic countries. In these politically oppressive environments, the *burca* and other forms of the veil become metaphors for hiding what is most feared. A woman then has no choice whether she wants to wear such a garment. The fear of betrayal is at the heart of this terrible imprisonment. Where Islamic extremists have held power, a woman dare not reveal her face, a lock of hair, a bare hand or ankle without severe punishment. Under the *Taliban* in Afghanistan, a woman would be stoned to death for being raped. It was also true under the regime of the Islamic Republic of Iran. Why such an awful reality can exist is a core question.

We need to be careful here, however. It is not just radical Islam that we see such severe reaction to women and fear of their independence. Throughout the world there are parallel reactions and restrictions on women's behavior. Radical Judaism and Christianity have carried their share of female repression. To deny this and point our religious and moral fingers at Islam is to mock our own histories.

We project onto other cultures and peoples what we are not able or willing to face in ourselves. We can say that Islam must hide the feminine behind forms of the veil because it is scared of something. But how are we, male or female, individual or culture, in any part of the world hiding behind our "*burca*" and "veil"? Of what are they made? How do we hide and thus confine the feminine principle? These questions may reveal our fear of life itself in its deepest and most intimate forms.

Classical Jungian thinking would describe the anima/feminine as the archetype of life itself as well as one's deep relationship to it. Is that what we are afraid of and is that what is projected unto women as a required destiny demanding to be fulfilled? Maybe this projection of life itself has its roots in the fundamental biological fact that a woman holds a child within herself for nine months, finally giving birth and nurturing her newborn in ways a man often finds hard to understand. Though she can carry and nurture life, she is not the archetype of life any more than another person is the archetype of death. Is archetypal life, that is, life in its most inclusive and fundamental form, what we fear woman will betray if she moves away from our projection of how she is to act? If so, then it would seem better to some to punish and even kill, if necessary, any woman who would threaten to dissolve that projection. To the person projecting onto her, she is the custodian of life itself and any sense of true meaning it could have. Yet, no individual or collective can sustain such a powerful projection without a defensive response that can take on explosive dimensions. This is why the Queens rebelled in such a dramatic manner. They betrayed their husbands because of how they dominated their kingdoms with one-sided masculine principles of inflexibility and oppression.

Though logical and the fuel for extreme fundamentalism in all three monotheistic religions—it's bad logic. The paradox here is that the more one tries to control an extreme position, the more one looses it. It is a tragic failure of the masculine world, be it in the masculinization of politics, education, or religion and, whether fostered by men or women, not to withdraw the literalizing projection onto women and eventually make possible the integration of the feminine principle in all aspects of our lives. For men specifically, it is a failure to look at, hold and honor the woman/en with her/their own soulful definitions. Devoid of that, power and the need to control will define a man's life. What men project onto women comes from their own successful or failed relationship to their inner feminine ground. About this Jung states: "Most of what men say about feminine eroticism, and particularly about the emotional life of women, is derived from their own anima projections and distorted accordingly."[44]

Metaphorically, and sometimes literally, the veil, used in an oppressive manner, covers our memories of the past of how we once were, our deepest longings for love and beauty and the terror of losing ourselves in them, our terror of dissolving in the power of sex, sensuality, beauty, relationships, earth, loss, death and ashes. Psychologically, the veil can be used as a dark projective metaphor by anyone to avoid looking deeply into themselves and turning away from the unknown, unfamiliar, or

---

44 C.G. Jung, *The Development of Personality*, CW 17, "Marriage as a Psychological Relationship" (New York: Pantheon Books, 1954), ¶ 338.

the stranger on the street. The veil can hide us from being honest with ourselves and open to understanding and meeting those who carry our projections. We can veil our views of God with prejudicial doctrinal garments defined according to our personal, political, and nationalistic needs. We veil our connection with the land by assuming Her at our disposal using up our "virgin" forests, our "virgin" prairie grasslands, our "virgin" water, air, etc. The question in more modern parlance is "What are we covering up?" or "What is so consequential that we dare not face it?"

It is perhaps for these reasons that the queen/s may have been contained and, for these reasons, she/they broke the imposed rules and, for these reasons, she/they were killed. The emphasis here is on "imposed rules" not on whether wearing a veil is a suppression of the feminine or not. An example of this difference is explained in Azar Nafisi's book, *Reading Lolita in Tehran*, (Random House, New York, 2003) in her reference to the Islamic revolution that took over her country:

> From the beginning of the revolution there had been many aborted attempts to impose the veil on women; these attempts failed because of persistent and militant resistance put up mainly by Iranian women. In many important ways the veil had gained a symbolic significance for the regime. Its reimposition would signify the complete victory of the Islamic aspect of the revolution, which in those first years was not a foregone conclusion. The unveiling of women mandated by Reza Shah in 1936 had been a controversial symbol of modernization, a powerful sign of the reduction of the clergy's power. It was important for the ruling clerics to reassert their

power. All this I can explain now, with the advantage of hindsight, but it was far from clear then.[45]

Nafisi makes it clear that wearing the veil is not the issue. Rather, the issue is the imposition of power, either from the clergy or political rulers that demand the feminine archetype be in service to them and their goals—rather than to Life. In that respect, the king confines the queen behind the palace walls under the delusion he is protecting *her honor*, when actually the out-of-control masculine is protecting *his power*. It is a confinement that is doomed to eventually fail as it did for the two brothers through betrayal.

The story of King Shahryar and his brother King Shahzaman hardly ends here, however. In fact, this is where the story begins. The reason this is so lies in the difference between grief and guilt on one hand, and shame on the other. If they had felt grief for the betrayal and loss of their wives, and guilt for what they had done, the story might have ended here. These are fundamental human experiences. We humans do betray one another, we make our mistakes, we get in the way, say things we should not, and do not speak when we should. There is loss throughout life. We lose relationships, jobs, youth, health, opportunities, levels of trust, and so forth. These are experiences that can either break or transform us, that can guide us along our individuation process, or derail us. Yet, in the end, they are still part of the fundamental processes of human drama. Shame, however, is what blinded the kings to these most fundamental of human experiences. Though shame is certainly a part of the drama of life, it has a far greater power to blind a

interesting?

---

45 Azar Nafisi, *Reading Lolita in Tehran* (New York, N.Y.: Random House, 2003), p. 112.

person to see what they must face. It can drive one from human community, if not literally, certainly intra-psychically.

This is what happened to the two kings. King Shahryar said to his brother Shahzaman: "Let us go hence and fare forth to seek our destiny upon the road of Allah; for we have no right in royalty, nor shall have, until we have found someone who has met a fate like ours: without that, in truth, death would be better than our lives."[46] This is a statement of shame; "we have no right to royalty." Their experience of shame was so profound there was no context great enough or human enough for them to explain or contain it in such a way that any felt sense of redemption from it was possible. They said, "We have no right in royalty, nor shall have, until we have found someone who has met a fate like ours." The task then was to find a context in which to place their shame in order to even stand a chance of being relieved of it. Until that time, death was preferable.

Are people willing to die because of unbearable shame? There is no doubt about this. Are people willing not only to die but also to kill because of shame? Again, it takes little imagination to know this is true. Shame is so powerful and profound, it takes a greater story to bring resolution. And so the story continues as they departed by a secret door of the palace, a fitting departure for one who is shamed.

It is said they traveled night and day until they came to a tree in the middle of a lonely meadow near the salt sea. Here they found an eyelet of water that refreshed them. This is a significant moment in the journey of the kings for it provides an opportunity to contain, face, and bring healing to their pain. The place to which they arrive is a *temenos*—a sacred and safe place. The ancient Greeks gave us this word. It referred to any place that was marked off, usually a temple of some God or Goddess.

---

46 *The Thousand Nights and One Night*, Vol. 1, p. 3.

In that place, a person was untouchable because it was a place of a divinity. Today we use the word "sanctuary." Psychologically, we speak of "feeling centered" or "needing to stand on our own ground" or "being secure in our own space." It is a worthy place to be but also a lonely one at times. A single tree in the middle of a lonely field suggests graphically how lonely this journey or recovery can be. It was for the kings. It was a lonely meadow near a salt sea. Though a "salt sea" might have been common in that part of the world, the fact that it is even mentioned then, might suggest it means more than a geographical location and have more to do with not yet felt, deep, unconscious grief. Regardless, it is a lonely meadow and is parallel to any moment in life when we are left alone with ourselves to face what only we can face. But it still remains a *temenos*.

The center of the world is where renewal happens. As in this story, there is often a tree that stands in the center. For the Germans it was the tree of Yagdrazil that Wotan hung on for nine days to gain wisdom; for the several tribes of the American Great Plains, it is the Sun Dance tree that becomes the center of all things for four days that holds the hope for the renewal of all life from year to year; for mystical Judaism it is the Sefirotic Tree that holds the formula for all life; and, then there is the Christian cross that is known as a tree that has been held as a symbol of transformation. It was in that lonely field that the opportunity was given and lost for the two kings.

When they rested, that is, finally let their guard down, a great apparition appeared in the form of a terrifying column of smoke and the appearance of a gigantic Jinni carrying a box on his head. A Jinn or Jinni is a spirit that can appear in human or animal form and is capable of doing good or evil to people. It was appropriate that the kings were terrified as it would be for anyone facing an archetypal moment in life, that is, when one is brought face to face with a power much bigger than the personal ego feels it is capable of handling. It is only natural to want to run away, build defenses, and retreat to our secure hiding places. Simply put, life can be frightening. What needs to be faced, however, usually does not go away. It did not for the kings, for here their journey provided them with an opportunity to put their shame into a larger context than the paralyzing effects it had caused.

The opportunity came when the Jinni took the box down from his head, opened it, and revealed a young woman, "shining like the sun."[47] This same woman was the Jinni's wife who betrays him while he slept and who shared with the kings her terrible experience of imprisonment on the night of her marriage. We now have an archetypal parallel to each of the two kings with their wives. The opportunity to place a mortal experience into archetypal context was before them. Here would be something bigger than either had experienced, a chance to be relieved of the feeling they were the only ones in history to have suffered like they had. To feel alone in our suffering in human history is too much to experience. It leaves us alienated from the rest of the human race and from any chance of finding our way back to a meaningful life. To realize that the drama we have experienced is archetypally coded into the human journey means we are not alone in that experience. Others have been there before us.

The parallels are striking. Each king had a wife that was contained behind the palace walls just as the Jinni contained his wife in a coffer, chained seven times and put at the bottom of the sea; each wife betrayed her husband while he was away just as the Jinni's wife betrayed him while he slept; each wife did what she wanted in her husband's absence as the Jinni's wife did what she wanted when he slept. And what they wanted was full

---

47 *The Thousand Nights and One Night*, p. 4.

sovereignty as a woman that included sexually erotic empowerment. It is this loss that is left out of the equation of what it is to be a woman in most parts of the world. Life wants its own erotic expression. It is this that is most feared by the masculine archetype out of control.

The story leaves no doubt of the Jinn's wife's desire to express her erotic nature. She says to them, "Come, pierce me violently with your lances" or she states, she will wake her husband who will kill them.[48] The erotic principle in woman demands to be awakened and honored. It is, however, not just the mortal woman that has suffered this loss and now struggles with these issues; it is the suppression of the feminine archetype or, what has been known mythically and theologically as the goddess. In the story, this can be seen in how the Jinni contained his wife in a chained box and placed it at the bottom of the sea. But, it was described as a sea that, "wars and dashes with its waves."[49] And that it should. When such a power as eroticism is contained for far too long, it can only erupt in violence and exaggeration. In the Western world, sex is seen everywhere, from TV to advertisements, to how we dress, in movies, magazines, and the proliferation of pornography on the web, etc. It is the goddess in her rawest form, obsessing us with what for too long we have not fully embraced, namely, the erotic nature of all life. We have weakened the place of Eros within the spiritual life of individuals and religious communities. In turn, because the monotheistic religions have had trouble incorporating the erotic into their theology, they suffer a spiritual sterility that frequently produces a deadening liturgy. Boredom is the end result.

48 *The Thousand Nights and One Night*, p. 4.
49 *Thousand Nights*, p. 7.

Eros draws one to the object in fascination, appreciation, and wonderment. It makes one want to relate to it, to look at it, to be in its world. It makes a person feel alive, vital, wanting to engage. When we speak of the erotic we think of sex; but, it is also more than sex. It is about life itself. Eros or, the erotic, is behind the force to create a song, write a poem, call a friend, sit quietly watching the bird feeder, as well as unashamedly admiring the beauty of the human body. The erotic is the magnetic force that draws us to one another and to the greater world. It also engages us with the darker issues of life. It makes us look at the realities of death, sickness, illness, and growing old. What an erotic moment it is when an old man or woman puts their arm around their dying spouse or friend, or when a parent suffers their child's illness. These are erotic moments that demand our attention and that cannot be avoided without severe consequences. Perhaps a softer word can be used here: sensual. Erotic and the sensual or sensuality are often blended together. The sensual has to do with the senses and the sensuousness that goes with them if we experience them through the world of soul. Sadly, we may look with our eyes but not see, we may hear but not listen, we may touch but not really feel, we may taste but not savor, or smell but not really remember.

Archetypally, the notion of a goddess or, in this case, the wife of a Jinni carries these life-giving powers. This whole story is about the suppressed feminine archetype and how this suppression affects the lives of human beings whether they be female or male. The kings defined their lives by containing their wives and later by what their wives had done to them with their betrayal. Never did the kings look at themselves except through the shame their wives caused them. Never mind that they violently killed their wives. The loss of the feminine archetype—or the absence of the goddess—gives us life without much soul. It sets us up to be far too objective with one another, far too judgmental, superficial in our relationships, and over-reliant on rules, mores, doctrines, and theories than with the soulful requirements of life often known as "common sense" or "doing the sensible thing" or being a "sensible, accepting, fun-loving human being."

This loss sets us up to look at one another as objects. When this gets translated into the workplace, employees become dispensable and oppressed with the demands of the "bottom line." When expressed in education we have: underpaid teachers with increasing demands placed upon them; disregard for the differences in ways children learn that are affected by cultural, racial, and socioeconomic factors; state of the art school buildings that do not match the end results of high standards of educational achievement.

This loss is reflected in politics in countless ways that generally support corporate survival over tackling the issue of unemployment, increasing health care costs that prevent people from getting the treatments they need, with little concern for the state of the environment, poverty, the state of most inner cities and so forth. Economically, it is reflected in our consumer mentality that has been raised to the level, of what we now call "globalization," creating markets that are sadly erasing small local businesses throughout the world.

It is obvious to see this suppression in the Middle East where radical Islamic men so easily and with moral justification can stone a woman for being raped; where holding hands can be severely punished; where women are required to wear full body cover including the veiling of their faces because of the dangerous power a woman has in seducing with her eyes.

It is less obvious to see this suppression in the Western world where literal forms of the veil are not required and death penalties are not imposed for such outrageous "crimes." Yet, the oppression and veiling still occurs archetypally in both women and men. In a masculine oriented culture, the anima usually takes a back seat to the ruling collective conscious environment.

Today, the feminine principle is returning worldwide with a demand for recognition. This is happening through the emerging power of women across the globe. Even in the most suppressive parts of the world women are fighting back. In her book, *Reading Lolita in Tehran*, Azar Nafisi, describes how a group of women under the repressive rule of the Islamic Republic of Iran defied dangerous consequences just to meet with her once a week to discuss literature that had been banned as immoral by the government. They wore "Western" clothes under their burcas and dared to wrestle with issues of freedom, women's rights, and their beloved Muslim religion, which was being damaged by extreme fundamentalists. In India, women are fighting back against bride burning, a practice which, though outlawed, is seldom prosecuted. In Somalia and other African counties where extreme forms of Islam thrive, groups of women are fighting back against female circumcision.

The feminine principle can no longer be contained or ignored. Even where such containment is still a reality, it cannot last for long. Though women are the first wave of people to feel the suppression and rise to the call of liberation, men are following. In the end, this is not a woman's issue—it is a human concern. No one flourishes with the feminine contained either behind a palace wall, in a box, or behind an imposed veil. Everyone suffers this loss. The Jinni's wife made it very clear. The kings were to come down from their false sense of safety high up in the tree, or, in analytic terms from the false sense of being individuated that comes with any fundamentalist position. They were to have sex with her but, put more symbolically, they were to take deep delight in the archetypal feminine and give her delight. They were to meet her on her terms. They were to engage her intimately and to experience the erotic at the most fundamental level—sex. As it turns out, they did to the Jinni what their wives' lovers did to them. We are back to betrayal. As their own wives made a bid for freedom from their own oppression, the Jinni's wife made her bid. She came alive, uncontained, demanding to be satisfied. This is fundamental to every human being. It is beyond gender. As the Goddess is a symbol of life, we are to satisfy Her, bring delight to Her and take delight from Her. Herein is our healing. If there is any doubt about the importance and power behind this, it is best summed up in what the Jinni's wife said of herself after she had described how she had been imprisoned in a box at the bottom of the sea: "But he did not know that whenever any one of us women desires a thing, nothing can prevent her from it."[50]

The story could have stopped here if the kings had only seen the parallel between their wives' containment and the Jinni's wife. Just as their wives simply wanted to be delighted in and empowered to be women in the fullest sense, so in the same manner the Jinni's wife demanded to be experienced and acknowledged to be the goddess woman she was. What a different story it would have been if the kings could have seen that they themselves betrayed their wives through disregard of their sovereign womanhood and, by default, betrayed the deeper archetypal feminine that they were now called on to obey. But they could not see these connections that had originally set the drama in motion. Instead of identifying with the suffering feminine, they identified with the Jinni—they could not escape the masculine grip.

Similarly, the two kings are in the same position of heading for a failed individuation when they said to each other: "If this be a Jinni and in spite of his power much more terrible things

---

50 *The Thousand Nights and One Night*, p. 5.

have happened to him than to us, it is an adventure which ought to console us."[51] Yet, as the story unfolds, it is obvious that they were not consoled. As soon as King Shahryar returned to his palace he, like his brother before him, killed his wife and his slaves, both men and women.

Thus far, this tale of two kings is a tale of two individuals being confronted with archetypal realities embodied in the Jinni and his wife. It is a confrontation of the personal with the impersonal, of one's limited truth with the greater truth. The cosmic couple of Jinni and wife are an expression of the masculine and feminine archetypes existing in an archetypal imbalance. One had suppressed the other. When the Jinni needed to sleep, the other, in this case the feminine, had a chance to come forth. She who had been contained finally had a chance to demand recognition and engagement on peril of death to those who disobeyed.

It takes little imagination today to see how this is reflected in many cultures throughout the world where the masculine archetype has dominated at the expense of the feminine. But where the masculine is losing its grip, where it is being culturally challenged, where it is willingly or unwillingly stepping aside, the feminine energies long held back are coming forth. This is the age of the emerging feminine archetype in the lives of both men and women. In our story here, the reference is the demand to pierce her with the lance, to bring pleasure to her, not to deny her. This all makes psychological sense if again we remember that, regardless of our gender, the king is a part of all of us—the king is the archetypal symbol of the conscious dominants that live our lives. Piercing the feminine may be just another way, albeit, a sexual way, of figuratively taking all of these masculine influenced dominants into the realm of the feminine mystery

---

51 *The Thousand Nights and One Night,* p. 5.

and truths of life that must stand alongside and equally participate in partnership with our kingly standards.

However, the kings' confrontation with these archetypal truths could not be personalized into their own lives back home. It is one thing to have an archetypal experience; it is another to integrate it into our personal lives. An example would be for someone to have a powerful experience of the sacred but not carry it back into all aspects of their personal life, instead picking and choosing how they will see its applicability. Even more problematic is when the experience is misused to fortify one's personal prejudice. In other words, one may miss the point of the whole story by choosing to focus on only a part of it. The kings did this. They could only identify with the plight of the Jinni and not of the injustice done to his wife. They could not step out of their own tale to see the greater story. Rather than seeing how they themselves had betrayed not just their wives but life itself in a fuller way, they used this archetypal drama to reinforce their own worldview of how they had been so betrayed.

Extreme fundamentalism, in any religion throughout the world, contains the experience of God within cultural, nationalistic, political, and personal dogmatic structures. The possibility of a greater worldview gets eliminated and those outside are judged with all the violent rhetoric that dominates our airwaves today.

It is not enough to say, "I had a religious experience" or "I had an archetypal dream last night." One must allow such experiences into the fullness of their life. This takes time and much reflection. This is where Sheherazade comes in. She is the mediator between the archetypal and the personal; between the greater story and its thousand and one expressions in personal history. Though the story talks about two kings, the focus is on one, who now is the representative of not only his brother but also of a kingdom in a state of killing the feminine in its virgin form.

The idea of "virgin" implies "unused" – "mine for the taking in all its newness" – "I will be the first." In other contexts, it can imply "in itself" or "sufficient unto itself"—thus, killing it is killing the "Other." Virgin killing in this story is psychologically similar to killing any new and fresh idea that is available to help individuate a person or culture. It is often played out for a while and made fun of later. Many creative and innovative movements in a culture fall to unfair criticism and jokes. This has been true of both the feminist and men's movements, various environmental issues, alternative medicine, and the world of religion itself. Feminists have been reduced to emasculating bra-burners; participants in the men's movement are viewed as men bonding and playing drums in the woods; environmentalists are defined as tree huggers; alternative medicine as quackery; and novel and pluralistic openness as watering down the essentials. The dismissive reactions of such innovative possibilities retard a culture from exploring the opportunities of ongoing creative advancement. Unless, that is, we remember a fuller history than our own particular era. The greater and longer history behind us has always moved from one idea to another. Every new idea ushered in change and, thus, often a struggle to further the evolutionary process of the culture involved. This struggle is required if life of any worth is to continue. Without change and the struggle that often accompanies it, a person and culture stagnates. Though major revolutions at times are required for cultural change, all cultures requires mini-revolutions in order to remain vital and nurturing. Respecting our history as a people and even as a planet, remembering the history that has brought us into the twenty-first century, might enable us to be less reactionary toward the mini-revolts and virgin-awakenings we experience. We might not "kill" them off so quickly if we could hear the story behind what ushered in their present cultural appearance.

Sheherazade was known for her studied ability to tell stories. Remember that it was said of her that she "had read the books, the annals, and the legends of old kings, together with the histories of past peoples. Also she was credited with possessing a thousand books of stories telling of the peoples, the kings, and the poets of bygone ages and of past time." The continual unfolding of story after story humanized the king and helped him see the greater truth of his archetypal experience of the Jinni's wife, which he and his brother had dismissed. As Sheherazade links him with the multifaceted dramas of human history, the king was able to reconnect with life. When the king killed woman after woman, night after night, he was killing his own anima soul. This is not only true of a man who denies his own feminine inner life, but also for both men and women in a culture such as ours today. Sheherazade redeems not only the killing of any more women in her country; she also redeems the king from his own madness and disconnection with life.

As early as one hundred and forty-five nights of storytelling into the thousand and one, the king begins to soften. He says: "As Allah lives, O Shahrazad, your little sister is right when she says that your words are delicious and savoury in their newness. I begin to regret having killed so many girls; it may even happen that I will forget my oath to make you share the fate of the others."[52]

Sheherazade tells the stories and is the Story. It took stories of the past to redeem the feminine and, eventually, the masculine principle from his hatred and alienation of life represented in woman. Sheherazade's knowledge of the past and

---

52 *The Thousand Nights and One Night*, Vol. 4, p. 582.

ability to humanize these stories bring the needed redemption. Her task is to keep the story going.

In the same way, we must keep the story going. Otherwise we hurt ourselves and one another simply because what mythically sustains us for a particular moment in history becomes too easily truncated and literalized, providing then the fuel that runs fundamentalism. This often occurs when there is fear of change, for example, with issues of race, gender, religion, and politics. In other words, cultural stories can easily be severed from any further development that occurs with the evolution of ideas from one generation to another. Sheherazade represents the feminine principle that keeps the story vibrant and animated. She is the continuing story. She represents the archetype of Life, and, as such, helps to move us from one story to the next, an evolutionary process that always intends to lead us to the next level of our individual or cultural history. Jung called this individuation. When our story gets stuck or stopped, problems develop. From a psychological perspective, this stuckness is known as neurosis or psychosis, both of which resist the notion of process. On a religious level it can be called extreme fundamentalism that fears change. When the story goes too fast, it is known psychologically as mania and religiously as blind excessive liberalism that has little respect for the natural flow of process. Sheherazade balances this tension, evolving the tales but at a pace that saves herself and eventually the king.

At the end of three years and a thousand and one telling of stories, the king's heart is changed. He says:

> O Sheherazad, that was a noble and admirable story. O wise and subtle one, you have taught me many lessons, letting me see that every man is at the call of Fate; you have made me consider the words of kings and peoples passed away; you have told me some things which were strange, and many that were

worthy of reflection. I have listened to you for a thousand nights and one night, and now my soul is changed and joyful, it beats with an appetite for life.[53]

It is then that she and her sister reveal the fruit of this "appetite for life." Dunyazad brings in twin babies and a crawling infant which were born to Sheherazade during these three years, unbeknownst to the king. She says:

> You remember, O King of time, that I was absent
> through sickness for twenty days between the six
> hundred and seventy-ninth night of my telling and
> the seven hundredth. It was during that absence that
> I gave birth to the twins. They pained and wearied me
> a great deal more than their elder brother in the
> previous year. With him I was so little disturbed that I
> had no need to interrupt the tale of Sympathy the
> Learned even for one night.[54]

The king responds, "O Shahrazad, I swear by the Lord of Pity that you were already in my heart before the coming of these children."[55] Then the king summons Sheherazade's father, his wazir, who feared continuously that his daughter would be killed. To him he says, "O father of Shahrazad, O begetter of benediction, Allah has raised up your daughter to be the salvation of my people. Repentance has come to me through her."[56]

Now the king summoned his brother, Shahzaman, who also had killed a virgin every night. Shahryar shared what he had experienced with Sheherazade, how his life had changed, which

---

53 *The Thousand Nights and One Night*, Vol. 4, page 531.

54 *Thousand Nights*, pp. 531-2.

55 *Thousand Nights*, p. 532.

56 *Thousand Nights*, p. 532.

touched Shahzaman's heart. In typical fairy-tale-like fashion, Shahzaman gives up his kingdom to Sheherazade's father and takes Dunyazad as his wife. Now two kings ruled together over one kingdom; two brothers married to two sisters.

The dramatic closure to the stories told over the course of a thousand and one nights powerfully portrays the healing effect of these stories. Where once the brothers had abandoned their kingdoms, killed their wives and slaves, sunk into grief, shame, and anger, leaving their kingdoms in near ruin for the diminishing feminine side of life, now there was reintegration of what had been split apart.

The structure of the story with two brothers having parallel lives suggests a division of identity, an inner conflict, as though the ruler were "of two minds." By story's end, however, the brothers became as one unit ruling one kingdom. Psychologically it is similar to a person saying, "Not only do I feel this way, but all of me feels this way"—not only the ego ground but every fabric of one's being. The union of the brothers is similar to anyone fully putting to rest the violence of any experience they might have had. This takes time and musing on many tales in one's mind to finally be able to feel any sense of healing. This is the work of the psychotherapeutic/analytic process where story after story, dream after dream can slowly and often unnoticed bring the sense that life can go on again. We can say we have moved on, but not uncommonly a trace memory will erupt, a parallel experience will open an old wound and we are back where we started if even for a brief moment. This is common to anyone who has been deeply violated.

Though one may never be completely cleansed of such memory, the metaphor of the union of two brothers ruling one kingdom suggests that a person's conscious life need not to remain divided from the inner world because of past trauma.

The union of two kings within one kingdom is similar to saying a person's inner and outer worlds are a psychological wholeness or "kingdom." The wisdom of the unconscious is dedicated to moving us along our individuation path. The birth of the three children to Sheherazade and King Shahryar reflects this progressive movement. Sheherazade, as the symbolic representation of Life, brought forth life through her children and through the telling of the needed stories all of which told of the multidimensional layers of life itself.

These stories were not neat. They were filled with complex relationships, intrigues, and high drama. But that's the point; they were stories about life—as life really is. The drive to make life neat, highly structured, and limited is where the story began: two kings each with a wife and servants behind palace walls, neatly contained but with life waiting to explode. And that it did. Locking away or placing a veil over life not only leads to an extreme fundamentalistic and myopic way of living, it proves to be psychologically and spiritually disastrous. A person trapped in this dilemma becomes unbearable to self and others.

Finally, we are told that the two brothers married the two sisters. Here is a powerful symbol of earthly wholeness. Now there are two kings and two queens. Two-ness implies depth, this and that, openness to different positions, I and Thou, arbitration, consideration, reflection, and balance. No longer is there a one-dimensional view of life; now we have perspective and openness to another side, another viewpoint, another person, another culture/politic/race/gender/religion. Who can stand alone today in a world that is struggling to maintain a continuity of life generated four billion years ago? Jung once said that the fate of the world today hangs by a very thin thread known as the human psyche.

Though the world is being torn apart today between East and West, North and South, the universality and timelessness of such stories as the *Thousand and One Nights* reflect healing forces that are always and simultaneously at work alongside forces that try to divide humanity. The task is to find and live those stories that are in service to life and to remember those stories that have gone before us—stories that can serve as templates for wise decisions and actions. Shahryar knew how important this was for himself and his people in order to avoid repeating those disastrous mistakes of his earlier life. It is written:

> Many faithful copies were made, and King Shahryar sent them to the four corners of his empire, to be an instruction to the people and their children's children.[57]

---

57 *The Thousand Nights and One Night*, Vol. 4, p. 536.

WORLDWIDE

Here or in India or in Africa
All things resemble each other.
Here or in India or in Africa
We feel the same love for grains.
Before death we tremble together.

Whatever tongue he may speak,
His eyes will utter the meaning.
Whatever tongue he may speak,
I hear the same winds
That he is gleaning.

We humans have fallen apart,
Boundaries of land split our mirth.
We humans have fallen apart,
Yet birds are brothers in the sky,
And wolves on the earth.

Fazil Husnu Daglarca[58]

TURKEY: BRIDGING EAST AND WEST

Turkey is a country that has the possibility of carrying the
polarities of East and West and becoming a bridge between two

---

58 Talat S. Halman, *Living Poets of Turkey* (Istanbul, Turkey: Dost
  Publications, 1989), p. 25

worlds. Turkey is the only country that straddles Europe and Asia. It borders on the west with Greece and Bulgaria, on the east with Georgia, Armenia, and Iran, and on the south with Iraq and Syria. Because of Turkey's location and the influence of two diverse populations, European and Asian, Turkey contains all polarities within herself. She has had a long and complicated history, incorporating the West and the East in religious and political affiliations. At the end of the Roman Empire, Constantine the Great brought Christianity to Turkey naming the city that became its center after himself, Constantinople. Eleven hundred years later the Ottoman army of Sultan Mehmet II captured the city, renamed it Istanbul and installed Islam as the country's official religion. The place that today is called Turkey shaped the beginnings of Christianity and was the last great empire of the Islamic world which ended as recently as the early twentieth century.

With the defeat of Germany at the end of the First World War, the victorious European allies began the division of the Ottoman Empire, parceling the desired parts for themselves. Mustafa Kemal, however, led the Turkish troops from Anatolia to the defeat of the European coalition, emerging with all the land intact and reversing the allocation of land awarded to Greece thereby creating the Republic of Turkey in 1922.

Kemal, later known as Ataturk, became the first president, setting the sights of Turkey, once again, to the West. Ataturk's vision was to build a democracy, become westernized, abolish the *caliphate* and dissolve Islamic courts and religious brotherhoods. Through military enforcement, he was able to tightly rule Turkey and dismantle the Ottoman's political and religious tradition. Ataturk singled out the veil as the object that must be eliminated, recognizing the symbolic significance both politically and religiously that it carried. Today, in Turkey, with an elected president still monitored by a council of Generals, the controversy continues about the wearing or not wearing the veil. Women are not allowed to wear the veil in public institutions or in Parliament. A striking example is Merve Kavakci who was elected as a minister of parliament in April 18, 1999, and was rejected from her seat on May 2 because she came wearing a headscarf. She was banned from politics for five years, and her citizenship was revoked. Today she teaches at George Washington University in Washington D.C.

The Kemalist generals continue to keep the spirit of Ataturk alive, driving Turkey towards westernization and the dream of joining the European Union. The West, however, has set human rights standards with which Turkey must comply in order to realize such a dream. As Ankara, the capital of Turkey, pushes West, the Turkish traditionalists and Islamists push back. Turkey wants to maintain its Islamic identity and its eastern traditions and, for many, that means not to over identify or cooperate at all with the West.

The women in Istanbul were seventy percent bareheaded and thirty percent covered in 2005. In the central and eastern parts of Turkey, women are rarely seen on the streets and wear head scarves in public. Younger, educated women wear head scarves as a political statement against Western ideology. These head scarves are called turbans, differentiating them from scarves in that they represent a political message. The tension between modern technology, economic potentialities, Western education and secular government and religion, family and tradition, shifts the focus from East to West and then East again in a continual competition for influence. The possibility exists that Turkey can be the bridge which holds together the values of the old and the new, integrating and transforming the nation and the world.

The authors of this book went to Turkey to research Muslim women's attitudes and came up with a list of questions. Turkey seemed to be the place where differences within both religious and secular opinions could be heard. How do women see America and American women? What about the Iraq war? What about Israel and American support of Israel or the secularization of Turkey, feminism, and the imposition of Western ideology on Islamic countries, especially Turkey? What about the heroine, Sheherazade, wearing the veil and trying to maintain Islamic identity in the face of Western culture? What was the perspective and thinking of Muslim women throughout the Islamic communities? What does America need to be aware of today, and how do they see the role of America in the world?

A woman agreed to be interviewed who lived in a fairy chimney house in Cappadocia. A fairy chimney house, also called a hoodoo, is a structure formed from sedimentary and volcanic rock formations found in the middle of Turkey in a conservative part of the country. She served apple tea and was most hospitable and felt privileged to be visited by Americans. She seemed to have been a good representative of the veiled women we interviewed in Turkey. A widow with three daughters, she works on a loom making carpets. Her adult daughter was visiting and visibly not wearing a headscarf. Her daughter is a college graduate and married. The first question asked was how she felt about her daughter's not having the same religious values. She said she was sad and that she told her three times to don the veil as Muhammad suggests her to do. Now it is up to her daughter and her relationship with Allah. However, she does not think the veil is the most important thing in the *Koran*. She has completed her task as a good Muslim mother. Her issues with American ideology have to do with family. Her perception of American parents is that they raise their children until eighteen years of age and then they are on their own. Muslim children are always the responsibility of parents and family. "No matter what, family is family." She doesn't believe in Western ideology because she thinks it will break up the family. She continues by stating that progressive women living in Istanbul, who are influenced by "modernism," become divorced and are struggling in the world of men. The rates of divorce in Istanbul are much higher than any other part of Turkey, up as high as forty percent. She thinks this is destroying the Muslim family. She had no problems with feminism as long as it does not contradict the messages from Allah. She believes there are differences between men and women, roles which one must obey and that, basically, women take care of the culture while "men cheat." She added that she doesn't like feminists who hate men.

interesting?

None of the women interviewed think that *Sharia* should be part of the government. Nor do those who wear scarves believe the government has the right to ban the wearing of scarves. The fairy chimney woman retells the story of another woman who was admitted to medical school, worked very hard, and then was told she could not graduate from medical school because she was wearing a veil. The woman committed suicide emphasizing the importance of being able to practice the religion that resonates with one's heart.

The Turkish women interviewed hate the state of Israel and believe Israel and the Jews of the world conspire to rule the world. America should not support Israel and believe America is being duped by Israel and manipulated into contributing support to meeting Israeli goals. These are but slices of the whole picture that are filled with negative projections held by Islamic women looking at the West.

To transform a country from one with internal conflict to a cohesive whole with all its differentiating parts, Sheherazade, the feminine who rescues the feminine and transforms the nation, must be invoked. The final and most inspiring interview was with a Muslim feminist woman who does not wear a head scarf, Halime Guner, general coordinator of a women's organization called the Flying Broom. Halime is an incarnation of Sheherazade in Turkey today. The United Nations Development Program and The International Women's Health Coalition support the Flying Broom. Halime Guner writes in the Flying News 1/2005:

> The Flying Broom was established nine years ago with the aim of increasing solidarity and cooperation by establishing a net of communication between women's civil society organizations and contributing to the strengthening of these organizations. We have realized several projects until today in order to spread gender equality awareness and to create sensitivities in this respect. Therefore, working for the development of democracy and civil society in Turkey has been our priority aim.[59]

Prior to the interview, Halime had just returned from a long trip to a town called Kars on the Georgian border where she was interviewing and educating the women of that area. There are 81 provinces in Turkey. The goal of the organization is to reach women in all those areas. These trips collect women's stories and concerns that are considered when forming new legislation and policies which affect women as well as telling their stories to raise public awareness. Just as Sheherazade tells the stories to transform a rigid, patriarchal king, the retelling of the women's stories brings consciousness to a nation, shaping something new. Flying Broom teaches women about human rights and how women can become more self-sustaining and protect themselves from abusive laws and traditions.

---

59 Halime Guner, "Flying News 3" (Woman's Communication Journal in *Flying Broom* magazine), (Ankara, Turkey: January 2005), p. 3.

Halime stated that most Turkish women want to join the European Union. Human rights benefits have already been enjoyed because of the EU's interest in Turkey. Women are aware there is more to be gained. Those women opposed to EU membership are generally more dependent and less educated. In a country where women are victims to honor killings and rape, the government, as of June 1, 2005, legalized an amended penal code that affects women's rights. With the help and education of Flying Broom, thirty out of thirty-six codes were changed to read that a violent crime against a woman is a crime against the injured individual instead of against the property of the family or society. The Flying Broom has influenced the establishment of a law on municipalities that support the opening of women's shelters in areas where the population exceeds 50,000 people. The importance of these shelters is based on research collected in September 2004 by the head office of Social Services Society for the protection of children and named "Violence against Women." Research sheds light on the power deferential between husbands and wives. Of 609 women, 24.6% experienced frequent violence. Another 15.5 % complained of a low level of violence. Shockingly, 51% of these women interviewed complained that their husbands did not need consent to have sexual intercourse.[60] In the West, we would consider this to be rape. Canan Arin, lawyer and founder of the Purple Roof Foundation for Battered Women, states, "Virginity testing forced in early marriages, honor killings will go on until women assumes the right to her own body."[61]

By creating a lobby for women, the Flying Broom has been supporting women for political positions of leadership in local elections. By the time of this interview, June 2005, the Flying

---

60 "Flying News 3," p. 19.
61 "Flying News 3," p. 27.

Broom had listed in their publication some of the following accomplishments that focus on educating women regarding human rights in a variety of mediums such as: (1) The civil society forum in Ankara where workshops are offered to women from all 81 provinces concerning women's rights; (2) the "Cedaw Handbook that served as a means of teaching women their rights in case they are subjected to discrimination was translated and published in multiple languages; (3) supported lobbying for women's organizations throughout Turkey; (4) has established a "local women's reporters network," an alternative media reporting on the local news about women and then transporting the local to national via website and publications; (5) and has created "Women 2004 Radio Program" in which academics, politicians, journalists and representatives from thirty-eight civil society organizations throughout Turkey all participated in telecasting for twenty-six weeks. The programming dealt with women's rights issues; (6) initiated the Flying Broom International Film Festival featuring women's films from around the world. The Flying Broom organization is exploring a variety of expressions to educate men and women in Turkey. An example is a photo exhibition on male roles which opened in 2005. In order for women to change, men have to change as well and learn to become more than the narrow roles they have been assigned. The organization continues to explore media and communication technologies to reach the vast Turkish populations for the purpose of transforming old unequal and rigid cultural norms into equal and powerful gender options within the Islamic and secular culture.[62]

Halime stated that most younger women are pro-Western, while middle-aged and older women are eastern in thought. She

---

62 Mehnet Ali Birand, *Turkish Daily News*, "Headscarf and Imam-hatip issues need to be resolved," June 24, 2005, p. 2.

said there are three different types of women in Turkey: those
that just embrace eastern ideology, those that are a combination
of eastern and feminist, and those looking West towards
inclusion into the EU and accepting Western attitudes. Women
represent the whole spectrum of thought, balancing extremes
and incorporating the whole. A new ideology is forming,
perhaps, as a model for the rest of the world. Turkey is proving
that the extremes between East and West may be able to
negotiate a third possibility where all ideas and resources can be
tolerated and appreciated.

When asked about women's attitudes to the West, Halime
stated that most of Turkey was sympathetic with America after
9/11, but that protest against America is on the rise. She went
on to say that American policies and relationships with other
countries are seen as aggressive. Turkey protests the war in Iraq
or invading any other country. She said that Turkey is making
strides in moving forward as America moves backwards. She
believes, as well as those she has spoken with, that America's
mission is about oil and not liberation. As a woman embracing
the value of wholeness and interconnection, Halime, a modern
day Sheherazade, would like to see the United States lead the
way for human rights and humanist policies. She believes
America has the power through education to improve humanity
as an alternative to employing the power of war. Her respect for
the American ideal of bringing consciousness to humanitarian
goals worldwide makes her believe that there could be one world
with America in leadership. Her vision of transformation is, "I
want power to be more lawful and equal to all humanity." Her
words are humbling to the King as noted in *The Thousand Nights
and One Night*.

The battle waged by Salahadin, the lesser *Jihad*, reduced the
outer threat of the West to Islam by defeating the Crusades. The
greater *Jihad*, the inner struggle, is a task suffered by all Muslims

resembling Jung's idea of individuation. The "other" within needs to be claimed making possible the incorporation of the whole. By other, we mean the parts of our shadow sides not recognized. The Prime Minister of Turkey, Erdogan (Her-Doe-Ahn) stands on a pro-Western platform in support of a secular democracy. However, as a devout Muslim whose wife wears a head scarf, he states: "Before anything else, I am a Muslim." He is the first prime minister since Ataturk who is leaning back to Islam. Thus, he is a representation of all Turkey, not just the Western version of Turkey. An editorial in the *Turkish Daily News* on June 24, 2005, addressed the head scarf debate as follows:

> … we need to satisfy the desires of those who see the head scarf beyond politics. Democracies are based on give and take. Agreements do not mean that one side has to give in to the other's demands. It does not mean we will turn a blind eye to acts that will change the path the country has chosen. Agreement means that both sides can go away with the knowledge they have achieved something for their sides. Thinking there is only one truth can only lead to acrimony and tension at a time when we cannot afford to fight.[63]

The head scarf debate continues to hold the symbol of secularism versus Islam. The debate offers the possibility of reuniting all the parts of the argument.

Sheherazade breaks the cycle of violence by embracing different terms of engagement. She is imaginative and reflective. She risks her life for the possibilities. Islamic countries other than Turkey, those and regimented by strict *Sharia*, perpetuate the past and stay locked in the complexes which rule their world. Extremists believe that *Sharia* cannot be changed; it is the word

---

63 Jan Goodwin, *Price of Honor*, (Boston, Massachusetts: Plume, 1995) p. 246.

of God, not man made. *Sharia* rule is different in each Islamic
country. Muslim feminists who support and appreciate *Sharia*
reason that its application should be relevant to contemporary
situations. Modified *Sharia* has raised the minimum age of
marriage, allows women to contribute financially to the
household, denies the ability to force underage marriages, gives
first wives the power to give consent for a second wife, limits
arbitrary divorce and allows women custody over children in
situations of divorce. An example of this version of *Sharia* is
Iraq, a secular Muslim country that has modified *Sharia* laws in
the following way: first, both men and women apply for divorce.
The law requires six months of counseling followed by a
decision at the discretion of the judge. Second, the mother is
granted custody of children in a divorce. Third, the father has
weekly visitation. Fourth, the father must leave his wife the
house and the car, and provide family support.

"Unless the woman is liberated there is no freedom in Iraq.
When the Iraqi woman is well, the Iraqi people are well and
when her position is disturbed, the disturbance reaches all the
Iraqi people."[64] Organizations with the intention of liberating
laws for women, thereby opening the tolerance of a whole
society, are in dialogue with clerics and governments to re-
interrupt *Sharia*. Islamic law inhibits and prohibits as well as
allows and encourages domestic tranquility. Sheherazade
illustrates that a woman's power is her capacity to think. *Sharia*
needs to be interpreted in a way that women can engage fully in
their culture and society. This participation increases the wealth
of resources available in the Islamic world.

Sheherazade does represent the capacity of the feminine
principle to think as well as remember the stories that unite all
people regardless of race, gender, religion, or economic and

---

64 Jan Goodwin, *Price of Honor*, p. 246.

educational differences. Though the full account of Sheherazade's *Thousand and One Nights* has middle eastern origins, one must ask where She is seen in the Western world. If her drama of liberation of the feminine principle and redemption of a king out of control has archetypal overtones, then this story like any such story regardless of origin can speak to all humanity.

Most generally speaking, though the names are different, Sheherazade is reflected in the entire feminist movement that has been going on for over a hundred and fifty years. Women have been speaking out, that is, telling the stories of injustice and the need for liberation in the full spectrum of life. The difference between Sheherazade and the king who loved her stories is that the dominant and dominating patriarchal world resisted the stories of leaders in the feminist movement often with physical and verbal violence.

The early suffragettes like Elizabeth Cady Stanton and Susan B. Anthony campaigned against slavery even before campaigning for women's rights. For what now seems so self-evident—that women worldwide have the same rights to equality before the law, in culture, politics, and economics—it's difficult to imagine the resistance to change during this earlier period. The point being that the stories needed to be told for the ongoing liberation of women and the feminine side of life and, indirectly, for the recovery of the patriarchy that had lost so much of its collective soul through excessive power, militarism, and disconnect from the environmental consequences of economic dominance.

These Western Sheherazade like stories were not easy to come by. Sheherazade incarnated in women like Virginia Woolf in her work *A Room of One's Own* or in Betty Friedan's book *The Feminine Mystique*. From the 1960s through the 1980s, there was the struggle for gender equality in laws and culture. Simone de

Beauvoir spoke of woman as the "other." Over time the feminist movement became increasingly successful because women in different situations developed their own ways and goals of feminism peculiar to their racial, ethnic and religious orientation. Today, women all over the world are speaking out, sometimes demanding to be heard, other times silently recreating a different story other than violence and revenge as in Rwanda where women from both sides of the conflict are meeting together in order to forgive and heal a nation that has experienced too much blood. From programs like Mothers Against Drunk Drivers, to Mothers of the Disappeared in Argentina who, for three decades, have fought for the right to reunite with their lost children and a woman like Ayaan Hirse Ali, who has, at the risk of her life, spoken out against the abuse of women in her native country of Somalia and those Somalian refugees who now continue to abuse women and young girls in her adopted home of Holland. Sheherazade cannot stop telling the stories either in the West or throughout the world. And the stories must continue because humanity as a whole still struggles to gain an awareness and consciousness of what it really means to be a human being. The original story of Sheherazade is titled *A Thousand and One Nights* because we are not there yet. The One Night means the story must go on because, as the poet, Fazil Husnu Daglarca, quoted at the beginning of this chapter says, "We humans have fallen apart."

Both East and West need to break out of rigid patterns of thinking and imagine something different. The Islamic projection of Americans as morally corrupt, socially degenerate, untrustworthy, ungodly, and "The Great Satan" is as intolerant and inflexible as the West's projections of Islam as fanatical, rigid, backward, primitive, and evil.

A new dialogue needs to emerge which can take back projections, unlock old patterns, and weave new stories. This takes the courage and imagination of Sheherazade to lift the veil of ignorance on all sides. Sheherazade represents the part of the psyche, the feminine, that is repressed and/or oppressed. Once her message is remembered and integrated, the whole is re-established, giving the psyche access to all its parts and establishing a sense of expansion and health, or, what Jung would call, an emergence of the Self. For a nation or culture to have access to the Self, its wholeness, it must unearth the complexes that shape the beliefs and attitudes of the society. In understanding what drives the emotions and laws of the day, a culture can begin to balance its internal process and have a fresh view of the external world and of other nations and cultures different from itself.

hope

Sheherazade commands with words not armies. Redemption begins with the dialogue between the powerful and powerless, bringing the feminine principle to the table of political debate to encourage self-determination and equality. Sheherazade offers a possibility of restoration. Through dialogue, the negative projections can begin to fall, providing the opportunity for each culture to be responsible for their own shadow. Once the defenses of projection are broken, the cultural ego can begin the grief work caused by prior trauma. A good example of that is America's need to grieve the losses of 9/11. At this point, the wholeness of the Lone Ranger would be manifested and his goal could now be realized, "I want to make this a safer place to live." The concept of wholeness would be re-established, reunifying all the disparate parts. The West and the East, in a partnership of diverse cultures, would need no longer to be dissociated and split off. Through the spirit of determined consciousness, each part of the divide would then be delivered from shame and powerlessness, integrating all parts into a new third.

Pro-Western Turkey must expand itself to include all its diversity. She is a living example of a culture that is growing psychologically to accommodate the whole. In her attempt to preserve the right to wear the veil, she is in fact lifting the veil towards greater consciousness. It is written in the *Koran, Sura* 13, line 11, "God does not change men's condition, unless they change their inner selves."

THE FUTURE

If all humans are intertwined and enfolded into a whole....
Kamerling

Early in his career, Jung introduced the concept of individuation to his developing theory of analytical psychology. It is a term meant to recognize and describe the lifelong process whereby one steadily grows into the uniqueness of who one was meant to be from the beginning of life. It implies a differentiation of consciousness from the social norm, on one hand, and the deep awareness of the undeniable connectedness with all humanity, indeed, with all of life on the other. It is to be an individual in the truest sense of the word, devoid of any individualism that isolates us from the world.

The intent of this writing has been to elucidate the underlying dynamics of the historical and present relationship between the Middle East/Islamic and Western/Judeo-Christian worlds using the perspective of Jungian psychology and the theme of the veil. We have seen that the events of today and certainly those that will unfold for a long time to come did not just happen in a vacuum. They are the result of longstanding cultural processes all too often grounded in wounds long in the making, coupled with major collective defenses of those very same wounds. The issues are deeply complicated by the use and misuse of religion for political motives, by excessive corporate power based primarily on the profit motive, and by govern-

122

mental machinations that appear to the observing world as inept and blind to the roles they play in furthering violence and poverty.

It is easy to weary that a solution to the violence will ever be found either in these two areas of the world or, for that matter, on a more global scale. "Just look around," one would say. Violence is not just experienced in the Middle East and its confrontation with the Western particularly North American world. It was not too long ago we saw the horror in Rwanda, apartheid in South Africa, the genocide in the Balkan countries and Darfur, the military threat in North Korea and Iran and the increasing anger in South American countries toward the United States. Human history has always been at war with itself. The World Bank, the World Monetary System, and the World Trade Organization have failed so often in their mission, fostered increased world poverty, and lowered the standard of living in third world nations while, at the same time, increasing their national debt. As for globalization, while it has brought goods to most any part of the world, it has also been responsible for the elimination of traditional products and ways of living. So what can we say about the future while these things are only the tip of the iceberg in the history of just the last one hundred years?

It is precisely at this point, however, that a person or a collective needs to make a decision. If indeed, it is hopeless, then that is the course we will set in the living of our lives individually and collectively. However, it was the late Jesuit priest and paleontological and evolutionary scientist, Pierre Teilhard de Chardin, who said that evolution, or, as is suggested here, individuation, is now taking place in the human psyche, and that we need to be cautious not to fall prey to two tendencies: isolation and discouragement. Isolation leads to separatism and racism. Discouragement gets us lost in hopelessness with no historical context. This inevitably results in the loss of our imagination for the future and creative hope of the human race as the next step in human consciousness. To not be cognizant of such an evolutionary process makes us lose perspective of the painful possibility that it might even be through our violence that we are raising human conscious to an awareness of what we do not want to have happen again. That, in fact, we might be moving toward a more differentiated and individuated time in history. Chardin puts it this way:

> Is the Universe utterly pointless, or are we to accept that it has a meaning, a future, a purpose? On this fundamental question Mankind is already virtually divided into the two camps of those who deny that there is any significance or value in the state of Being, and therefore no Progress; and those, on the other hand, who believe in the possibility and the rewards of a higher state of consciousness.[65]

As hard as it may be to believe in such a process leading toward the future, it is just that which is required. Knowingly, or not, when individuals undergo an individuating process, so do cultures and nations. We need to challenge any traces we may have of jaded opinions of just what the world is capable of humanely becoming. Maybe the world itself, beyond nation states, is individuating toward what Jung referred to as the *Unus Mundus,* that is, the One World. Chardin said that the world itself even more than individuals has a soul that needs to be redeemed. That is the central task of this new century.

The world is changing fast today, faster than ever before in human history. This is due primarily to the Internet and fiber optic cable that in a nanosecond can connect anyone to nearly any part of the world. What once took decades or even centuries

---

65 Pierre Teilhard Chardin, *The Future of Man* (New York and Evanston: Harper & Row, 1964), p. 42.

to achieve, now can happen or change overnight. We are in the era of major shifting paradigms. This can all be seen under the rubric of the individuating process of a nation or culture. As with any individual journey through life, the process is difficult. It is beset with countless struggles or what can be called complexes that demand attention. As has been stated, every culture has complexes that are a part of the individuating history of that collective. This is inevitable. Yet, complexes collectively enacted, discovered, and consciously faced become the way a culture discovers itself.

However, the biggest issue today is beyond nation states. It is now required to identify and give clarity to worldwide complexes. For example, it is now common to speak of globalization, global warming, global economy, global terrorism, and global communication. These issues are beyond any one culture. They involve everyone in every corner of the planet. The world is getting more and more compressed not only by population growth but also by our growing awareness of one another. The person who will help us with our technical problems is not down the street but on the other side of the world. The notion of globalization, for example, can expand beyond particular concern for economic and local trade struggles to a more noble but complicated possibility of global consciousness. Or, to put it more pragmatically, there are very few individual nation states that can isolate their political problems from the rest of the world. Here is globalization in a whole new context: globalization of the human spirit that brings with it all of its noble and ignoble possibilities. It is already happening. Where can anyone hide today? The world is struggling to evolve, to ascend to a planetary awareness of a better day, an awareness which we are capable of attaining but just as capable of not. Here, there is no guarantee, only the possibility. Here any notion of "lifting the veil" in order to shed the light of consciousness on collective destructive motives as well as awareness of a new humanity moves beyond Western and middle eastern conflicts to include the entire world.

What is required, however, is that neither an individual nor a culture should deceive itself with naiveté or with any form of New Age sentimentality. New eras are almost always ushered in by violence, disturbance of the cultural norms, fanaticism, and fatal attempts to hang on to a way of life that has now run its course. This phenomenon is what the world is experiencing at the beginning of the twenty-first century. What is required in this time is serious reflection and avoidance of simple or reactionary answers.

Carl Jung referred to the German word '*Weltanschauung*" to describe what is referred to here as the paradigm or paradigms that overlay a culture. It is like an umbrella of norms, mores, worldviews, and values that structure or affect anyone's life within that collective. But every *Weltanschauung* needs to evolve or individuate. Jung says:

> Consciousness determines *Weltanschauung*. All conscious awareness of motives and intentions is a *Weltanschauung* in the bud; every increase in experience and knowledge is a step in the development of a *Weltanschauung*. And with the picture that the thinking man fashions of the world he also changes himself. The man whose sun still moves around the earth is essentially different from the man whose earth is a satellite of the sun. In short, it is not a matter of indifference what sort of *Weltanschauung* we possess, since not only do we create a picture of the world, but this picture retroactively changes us.[66]

---

66 C.G. Jung, *The Structure and Dynamics of the Psyche*, CW 8, "Analytical Psychology and Weltanschauung" (New York, N.Y.: Pantheon Books, 1960), ¶ 696.

And again:

> If the picture we create of the world did not have a
> retroactive effect on us, we could be content with any
> sort of beautiful or diverting sham. But self-
> deception recoils on us, making us unreal, foolish,
> and ineffectual. Because we are tilting at a false
> picture of the world, we are overcome by the
> superior power of reality.[67]

And finally:

> The fatal error of every *Weltanschauung* so far has
> been that it claims to be an objectively valid truth....
> This would lead to the insufferable conclusion that,
> for instance, the same God must help the Germans,
> the French, the English, the Turks, and the heathen
> —in short, everybody against everybody else.[68]

or with?

What this book has attempted to describe is how cultural
wounds and the archetypal defenses of the group spirit, be they
of the Middle East or of the Western powers, add to the spirit
of the age in which we live. The existing paradigms or, in Jung's
word, the *Weltanschauung,* determines our response to the world.
We cannot escape its influence; our only hope is in struggling to
become as conscious as we can of what is living us.

It is precisely here that we need the Sheherazades of the
world to remind us of our stories long past but forgotten. We
need to see how we have emerged and individuated over time
and to remember what once nourished us spiritually and
protected us from our own self-deceit as well as challenged us to
continually define and redefine our lives individually and

---

67 C.G. Jung, *The Structure and Dynamics of the Psyche*, CW 8, ¶ 699.
68 C.G. Jung, *The Structure and Dynamics of the Psyche*, CW 8, ¶ 734.

collectively. Here we might also discover where our story stopped, where the individuation process got truncated through indifference or severe trauma and by the suppression of the feminine principle.

For the stories to revive and for new stories to emerge requires a return of the eternal feminine on a full worldwide scale. It is to lift the veil on the way the world has been influenced by an overpowering masculine archetypal energy that must progress at all cost regardless of the welfare of local communities, nation states, or the environment. Masculine energy out of control only happens when it is not balanced by a counter but cooperative force known generally as the feminine principle. Though the feminine principle is showing signs of returning, it is met with massive resistance as witnessed in the battles between environmentalists worldwide and those who depend on the exploitation of coal and oil for their profits. One side considers what ancients have called "Mother Earth" and the other is dedicated to the god of progress and wealth.

A thorough and consistent study of world history can continue to unearth the processes that brought any nation or culture into the present time. The raging of the Middles East, its increased resentment and anger at North America in particular and the increase in terrorism can trace its roots back generally to Muhammad and particularly to the way the Western powers divided up this vast land after the fall of the Ottoman Empire. To learn more of world or Middle Eastern history would help anyone to understand "why they hate us." It did not happen in a vacuum.

So, Sheherazade is our historian. She is that desire in any one of us to look back and try to understand our individual and collective stories. She is that animated force behind psyche's demand to bring not just the memory but also the lessons of our histories into the political decisions we make now and in the future. She is that drive in us to stay alive in the age of the raging kings that would kill anything that would smack of life. In a moment of sarcasm, Jung states:

> ...heaven preserve us from psychology—that depravity might lead to self-knowledge! Rather let us have wars, for which somebody else is always to blame, nobody seeing that all the entire world is driven to do just what all the world flees from in terror.[69]

We have the ability to stay consciously alive and informed today as never before on the web, in film, in literature, in documentaries, and through the courageous efforts of thinking individuals and small groups who challenge the status quo. Stories that last are grounded on archetypal themes applicable to all people everywhere. But it is up to each generation to clarify what it is saying to its time. We must not make ourselves and others victim by claiming that our *Weltanschauung* is an "objectively valid truth." Such a truth, as Jung stated, "...recoils on us, making us unreal, foolish, and ineffectual." Otherwise, we take ourselves too seriously and make the mistake of confusing our "little stories" with the Great Story embedded in the timeless flow of humanity's journey.

In every sense, this book has been about exposure of the collective neurosis, an admittedly limited attempt to lift the veil on cultural complexes on both sides of the world in order to facilitate the individuation of our collectivities and to push the story forward. But when the king rages, when war happens, there are always "us" and "them" with all of the initial glory and

---

69 C.G. Jung, *The Archetypes and the Collective Unconscious*, CW 9, 1, "The Phenomenology of the Spirit in Fairy Tales" (Princeton, N.J.: Princeton University Press, 1959), ¶ 454.

nationalistic fervor of the struggle only to yield to the hubris, inept decisions and fateful tragic endings. No nation is just a victim or just a perpetrator. Political decisions based on such a paradigm of limited perspective only lead to the dehumanizing of both sides while, at the same time, reinforcing those cultural complexes that fuel our projections onto the "other." There will always need to be an "other," someone to blame for our sad state of affairs, someone that represents the threat to our supposed progress and stability of our country or culture. There will always be elements of truth behind the accusations of the "other" but, when propagandized to the extreme, the end result is the dimming of consciousness. And there will always be the struggle to withdraw projections.

As of this writing, a new president resides in the White House who is a mixture of cultures. He describes himself as a black Christian man, raised for several years in his youth in Indonesia, a Muslim country. He perceives himself as a bridge maker. On June 4, 2009, he spoke to a Muslim audience at Cairo University in Cairo, Egypt. This was his first visit to an Islamic theocracy since his inauguration the previous January. He states:

> We meet at a time of tension between the United States and Muslims around the world—tension rooted in historical forces that go beyond any current policy debate. The relationship between Islam and the West includes centuries of co-existence and cooperation, but also conflict and religious wars. More recently, tension has been fed by colonialism that denied rights and opportunities to many Muslims, and a Cold War in which Muslim-majority countries were too often treated as proxies without regard to their own aspirations. Moreover, the sweeping change brought by modernity and globalization led many Muslims to view the West as hostile to the traditions of Islam.

Violent extremists have exploited these tensions in a small but potent minority of Muslims. The attacks of September 11th, 2001 and the continued efforts of these extremists to engage in violence against civilians has led some in my country to view Islam as inevitably hostile not only to America and Western countries, but also to human rights. This has bred more fear and mistrust.

So long as our relationship is defined by our differences, we will empower those who sow hatred rather than peace, and who promote conflict rather than the cooperation that can help all of our people achieve justice and prosperity. This cycle of suspicion and discord must end. I have come here to seek a new beginning between the United States and Muslims around the world; one based upon mutual interest and mutual respect; and one based upon the truth that America and Islam are not exclusive, and need not be in competition. Instead, they overlap, and share common principles – principles of justice and progress; tolerance and the dignity of all human beings.

I do so recognizing that change cannot happen overnight. No single speech can eradicate years of mistrust, nor can I answer in the time that I have all the complex questions that brought us to this point. But I am convinced that in order to move forward, we must say openly the things we hold in our hearts, and that too often are said only behind closed doors. There must be a sustained effort to listen to each other; to learn from each other; to respect one another; and to seek common ground. As the Holy *Koran* tells us, "Be conscious of God and speak always the truth." That is what I will try to do – to speak the truth as best I can, humbled by the task before us, and firm in my belief that the interests we share as human beings are far more powerful than the forces that drive us apart. Of course, recognizing our common humanity is only the beginning of our task. Words alone cannot meet the needs of our people. These needs will be met only if we act boldly in the years ahead; and if we understand that the challenges we face are shared, and our failure to meet them will hurt us all.[70]

President Obama advocates understanding and the retelling of cultural stories to connect two conflicting worlds. Within his speech, he acknowledges the historical tensions that have existed between the Western and Islamic worlds as well as challenging both to cooperatively contribute to the emergence of new relationship. He discusses violent extremism and its destructive ramifications. He continues his speech with a discussion about the conflict between the Palestinians and Israelis and says America will support the peacemaker. He acknowledges nuclear weapons as a problem for all peoples and is hopeful nuclear proliferation will be totally eliminated by all nations. He believes all nations have the right to chose their own style of government, democratic or not and fosters economic development and opportunity throughout the world. He opens a dialogue regarding cultural differences and encourages the joining together on our commonalities. Obama recognizes the whole when he states:

> For we have learned from recent experience that when a financial system weakens in one country, prosperity is hurt everywhere. When a new flu infects one human being, all are at risk. When one nation pursues a nuclear weapon, the risk of nuclear attack rises for all nations. When violent extremists operate

70 Obama, Barack, *Remarks By The President On A New Beginning*, Cairo University, Cairo, Egypt, June 4, 2009.
http://www.whitehouse.gov/the-press-office/remarks-president-cairo-university-6-04-09

in one stretch of mountains, people are endangered across an ocean. And when innocents in Bosnia and Darfur are slaughtered, that is a stain on our collective conscience. That is what it means to share this world in the twenty-first century. That is the responsibility we have to one another as human beings.

This is a difficult responsibility to embrace. For human history has often been a record of nations and tribes subjugating one another to serve their own interests. Yet, in this new age, such attitudes are self-defeating. Given our interdependence, any world order that elevates one nation or group of people over another will inevitably fail. So whatever we think of the past, we must not be prisoners of it. Our problems must be dealt with through partnership; progress must be shared. That does not mean we should ignore sources of tension. Indeed, it suggests the opposite: we must face these tensions squarely.[71]

President Obama appreciates the power of the symbol. He criticizes Western countries that try to control the practice of wearing the veil and warns against,

.... dictating what clothes a Muslim woman should wear. We can't disguise hostility towards any religion behind the pretense of liberalism.

I know .... there is a healthy debate about this issue. I reject the view of some in the West that a woman who chooses to cover her hair is somehow less equal, but I do believe that a woman who is denied an education is denied equality. And it is no coincidence that countries where women are well-educated are far more likely to be prosperous.

71 Obama, Barack, June 4, 2009.

Now let me be clear: issues of women's equality are by no means simply an issue for Islam. In Turkey, Pakistan, Bangladesh, Indonesia, we have seen Muslim-majority countries elect a woman to lead. Meanwhile, the struggle for women's equality continues in many aspects of American life, and in countries around the world.

.... our daughters can contribute just as much to society as our sons, and our common prosperity will be advanced by allowing all humanity—men and women—to reach their full potential. I do not believe that women must make the same choices as men in order to be equal, and I respect those men who choose to live their lives in traditional roles. But it should be their choice. That is why the United States will partner with any Muslim-majority country to support expanded literacy for girls, and to help young women pursue employment through micro-financing that helps people live their dreams ....

All of us share this world for but a brief moment in time. The question is whether we spend that time focused on what pushes us apart, or whether we commit ourselves to an effort – a sustained effort – to find common ground, to focus on the future we seek for our children, and to respect the dignity of all human beings.[72]

Obama challenges the world to lift the veil of ignorance and allow all the freedom to choose their cultural perspective. Women carry a measure of psychological consciousness within a society. A progressive society that provides equality for women is a successful society for all its citizens.

President Obama's closing of his Cairo speech can serve as an inspiring summation for this book:

---

72 Obama, Barack, June 4, 2009.

It is easier to start wars than to end them. It is easier to blame others than to look inward; to see what is different about someone than to find the things we share. But we should choose the right path, not just the easy path. There is also one rule that lies at the heart of every religion – that we do unto others as we would have them do unto us. This truth transcends nations and peoples – a belief that is not new; that is not black or white or brown; that is not Christian, or Muslim, or Jew. It is a belief that pulsed in the cradle of civilization, and that still beats in the heart of billions. It is a faith in other people, and it is what brought me here today.

We have the power to make the world we seek, but only if we have the courage to make a new beginning, keeping in mind what has been written.

The Holy *Koran* tells us, "O mankind! We have created you male and a female and we have made you into nations and tribes so that you may know one another.

The Talmud tells us: "The whole of the Torah is for the purpose promoting peace."

The Holy Bible tells us, "Blessed are the peacemakers, for they shall be called sons of God."

The people of the world can live together in peace. We know that is God's vision. Now, that must be our work here on Earth.

Thank you. And may God's peace be upon you.[73]

Regardless of one's political or religious orientation, President Obama's speech is a challenge and call to everyone everywhere. It is a speech that reflects an emerging vision that is awakening in the hearts of people worldwide. He challenges the

73 Obama, Barack, June 4, 2009.

potential in all of us to work for the evolution of a worldwide consciousness that recognizes and respects the inter-connectedness of all humanity in a world that is growing smaller. There are no promises only the belief that the world we know, coupled with determination and hard work, can eventually be a world at peace with itself.

Ultimately, the most deadly veil is the veil of self-delusion that divides us from the rest of life. Though this book has focused primarily on the inter-relational psychological dynamics between the Middle East and the Western world, the metaphor of the veil is far more inclusive. It must now be seen as a planetary phenomenon. It is the veil that has covered the world itself, a veil that has hidden us from one another, weakened our sense of responsibility to our own specific domicile and the health of the entire planet.

GLOSSARY

abaya - A black coat with arm slits that falls from the top of the head to the ankles. Persian Gulf countries.

Allah - God

Andarun - The women's quarters.

Ayatollah - The reflection of God.

Burca/Burka/Burqa - A face mask made of leather or stiff fabric covers entire face except eyes. Seen in Gulf countries.

Caliph - A successor to the prophet Muhammad. Literally, one who comes after.

Caliphate - The institution of Islamic government.

Chador - A square of fabric that falls from the top of the head to the ankles, held closed under the chin. Iran and Lebanon.

Fatwa - A legal opinion of decision on religious law.

Fatiha - The opening prayer said 5 times a day.

Hadith - A saying of the Prophet Muhammad or a saying about him by his contemporaries.

Hajj - A pilgrimage to Mecca required of all Muslims once in a lifetime.

Hijab - Literally means curtain. Dress that follows Islamic principles.

Harem - It means forbidden, where women reside.

Hijrah - The journey from Mecca to Medina – July 16, 622.

Imam - The leader of community prayers.

Islam - It literally means submission.

Islamic Salvation Front - A Muslim liberation organization – Algeria.

Ijtihad - The independent reasoning used by a jurist to apply *Sharia* to contemporary circumstances.

Jahiliyya - The age of ignorance—used for pre-Islamic period and today to describe societies not Islamic.

Jalabiyya - A neck to ankle coat worn by women; a loose fitting robe worn by men.

Jihad - The holy effort of struggle; war to defend Islam.

Ka'ba - A structure built by Adam, rebuilt by Abraham with Ishmael—the most sacred mosque in Mecca.

Koran - (also spelled *Qur'an*) It literally means to recite. The holy book of Gods message to Muhammad—written 650 A.D.

Madrassa - An Islamic school.

Meuzzin - One who sings the call to prayer.

Mujahedin - Muslim fighters in Afghanistan.

Mullah - A clergyman—religious leader.

Muslim - It literally means "one who submits."

Niquab - A veil that completely covers the face.

Purdah - A screen or curtain used to keep women separate from men or strangers thus keeping women in seclusion.

Rashidun - The four "rightly guided" caliphs, successors of Muhammad: Abu Bakr, Umar ibn Al-Khattab, Uthman ibn Affan and Ali ibn Abi Talib.

Roosarre - A head scarf—Iran.

Salwar-kameez - A tunic worn over pants—India, Pakistan.

Sharia - It literally means "road to the water" referencing Islamic law.

Shehada - The first pillar of Islamic religion.

Shiite - A group developed in seventh century over a controversial split of who should be *Caliph*. The *Shi* are followers of Ali ibn Abu Taleb, Muhammad's cousin and son-in-law (husband to Fatima, the prophet's daughter), believing he was the legitimate successor of Muhammad because he was a descendant of the prophet. They are the majority in Iran, Iraq, Dubai and Bahrain; otherwise, they are the minority in other Muslim countries.

Sunnah - The traditions of the prophet—his behaviors, approved of behaviors, and actions done in his presence without disapproval.

Sunni - It literally means one who follows Muhammad's tradition or orthodox Muslim.

Sura/Surah/Surat - A division in the *Koran*. It can be approximately referred to as a paragraph or chapter, although these terms are sometimes avoided, as the suras are of unequal length.

Taloq - It means divorce. A husband announces he wants a divorce three times and the divorce is done.

Ulema - Religious scholars who interpret Islamic law.

Ummah - The Muslim community worldwide.

Wahabism - A puritanical, ultraconservative movement founded in 1740s in Saudi Arabia by Muhammad ibn Abdul Wahab. Women are denied many rights because of strict interpretation of *Koran* and *Hadith*.

Zakkat - Charity, a requirement of the 5th pillar.

BIBLIOGRAPHY AND SUGGESTED READINGS

Ahmed, Leila. *Women and Gender in Islam*. New Haven & London: Yale University Press, 1992.

Ali, Ahmed. *Al-Qur'an*. Princeton, N.J.: Princeton University Press, 2001.

Armstrong, Karen. *The Battle for God*. New York: Random House, 2000.

Armstrong, Karen. *Islam*. New York: The Modern Library, 2002.

Armstrong, Karen. *Muhammad*. New York: Harper San Francisco, 1992.

Armstrong, Sally. *Veiled Threat: The Hidden Power of the Women of Afghanistan*. New York: Four Walls Eight Windows Press, 2002.

Beebe, John (Edited). *Terror, Violence and the Impulse to Destroy*. Einsiedeln, Switzerland: Daimon Verlag, 2003.

Brooks, Geraldine. *Nine Parts of Desire: The Hidden World of Islamic Women*. New York: First Anchor Books, 1996.

Campbell, Joseph. *Arabian Nights*, New York: Viking Press, 1967.

Cooley, John. *Unholy Wars*. London and Sterling, Virginia: Pluto Press, 2000.

Desai, Anita. *The Turkish Embassy Letters*. London: Virago Press, 1994.

Goodwin, Jan. *Price of Honor*. Boston, Massachusetts: Plume, 1995.

Guner, Halime. "Flying News 3, Women's Communication Journal." in *Flying Broom* magazine: Ankara, Turkey 2005.

Halman, Talat S. *Living Poets of Turkey*. Istanbul, Turkey: Dost Publications, 1989.

Hertz, Noreena. *The Silent Takeover*. New York, London: The Free Press, 2001.

Hillman, James. *A Terrible Love of War*. New York: Penguin Press, 2004.

Hourani, Albert. *A History of the Arab Peoples*. New York: MJF Books, 1991.

Jones, James W. *Terror and Transformation*. New York: Brunner-Routledge, 2002).

Jung, C.G. *Symbols of Transformation*, C.W. 5. Princeton, N.J.: Bollingen Series, Princeton University Press, 1956.

Jung, C.G. *Psychological Types*, C.W. 6. Princeton, N.J.: Bollingen Series, Princeton University Press, 1971.

Jung, C.G. *Structure and Dynamics of the Psyche*, C.W. 8. New York, NY: Bolligen Series Pantheon Books, 1960.

Jung, C.G. *Archetypes and the Collective Unconscious*, C.W. 9, 1. Princeton, N.J.: Bollingen Series, Princeton University Press, 1959.

Jung, C.G. *Mysterium Coniunctionis*, C.W. 14. Princeton, N.J.: Bollingen Series Princeton University Press, 1970.

Jung, C.G. *The Development of Personality*, C.W. 17. Princeton, N.J.: Bollingen Series Pantheon Books, 1954.

Kalsched, D. *The Inner World of Trauma: Archetypal Defenses of the Personal Spirit*. London and New York: Routledge 1996.

Khalidi, Rashid. *Resurrecting Empire*. Boston, Massachusetts. Beacon Press, 2004.

Kinzer, Stephen. *All the Shah's Men*. Hoboken, N. J.: John Wiley & Sons, 2003.

Kinzer, Stephen. *Crescent and Star*. New York: Farrar, Straus & Giroux, 2002.

Lane, E.W. and Poole, E.S. *The Thousand and One Nights: Commonly Called, in England, The Arabian Nights' Entertainments*, Chatto and Windus, 1839. Available from http://www.books.google.com as a free ebook.

Lewis, Bernard. *The Crisis of Islam*. New York: Random House, 2004.

Logan, Harriet. *Unveiled*. New York: Regan Books, 2002.

Lunde, Paul. *Islam*. London, New York, Munich, Melbourne, Delhi: DK Publishing, 2002.

Mai, Mukhtar. *In The Name of Honor*. New York: Atria Books, 2000).

Mathers, Powys. *The Thousand Nights and One Night*, (4 Volumes). New York: St Martin's Press, 1972.

Menocal, Maria Rosa. *Ornament of the World*, Boston, New York, London: Little Brown and Company, 2002.

Mernissi, Fatima. *Beyond the Veil*, Cambridge, Massachusetts: Schenkman Publishing Company, Inc., 1975.

Mernissi, Fatima. *Sheherazade Goes West*. New York & London: Washington Square Press, 2001.

Milton-Edwards, Beverly. *Islamic Fundamentalism Since 1945*. London & New York: Routledge, 2005.

Morgan, Robin. *The Demon Lover*. New York: Washington Square Press, 1989.

Nafisi, Azar. *Reading Lolita in Tehran*, New York: Random House, 2003.

Obama, Barack. *Remarks By The President On A New Beginning*, Cairo University, Cairo, Egypt, 2009. http://www.whitehouse.gov/the-press-office/remarks-president-cairo-university-6-04-09

Qutb, Sayyid. *In the Shade of the Qur'an*, New Delhi, India: Islamic Book Service, 2001.

Rauf, Imam Feisal Abdul. *What's Right with Islam*, New York: Harper San Francisco, 2004.

Regan, Geoffrey. Lionhearts, Richard I, *Saladin and the Era of the Third Crusade*. Walker Publishing Co. Inc.,1998.

Roald, Anne Sofie. *Women in Islam*. London & New York: Routledge, 2001.

Roy, Oliver. *Globalized Islam*. New York: Columbia University Press, 2004.

Sabbagh, Suha,(editor). *Arab Women*. New York: Olive Branch Press, 1996.

Singer, Thomas. "The Cultural Complex and Archetypal Defenses of the Collective Spirit: Baby Zeus, Elian Gonzales, Constantine's Sword, and Other Holy Wars." *The San Francisco Jung Institute Library Journal*, Vol. 20, No. 4 (2002), pp. 5-28.

Singer, Thomas. "Unconscious Forces Shaping International Conflicts: Archetypal Defenses of the Group Spirit from Revolutionary America to Confrontation in the Middle East." *The San Francisco Jung Institute Library Journal,* Vol. 25, No. 4 (2006), pp. 6-28.

Singer, Thomas & Samuel Kimbles. *The Cultural Complex.* New York: Brunner-Routledge Hove, 2004.

Stiglitz, Joseph, *Globalization and Its Discontents.* London: W.W. Norton Company Ltd., 2003.

Sulaiman, Kalid. *Palestine and Modern Poetry.* London: Zed Books Ltd., 1984.

Swarup, Ram. *Understanding the Haddith.* New York: Prometheus Books, 2000.

Syed, Muhammad Ali. *The Position of Women in Islam.* New York: State University of New York Press, 2004.

Von Franz, Marie-Louise. *The Interpretation of Fairy Tales.* New York: Spring Publications, 1970.

Viorst, Milton. *In the Shade of the Prophet,* Boulder, Colorado: Westview Press, 2001.

Zola, Luigi & Donald Williams. *Jungian Reflections on September 11.* Einsiedeln, Switzerland: Daimon Verlag, 2002.

ABOUT THE AUTHORS

Jane Kamerling, L.C.S.W. is a Diplomate Jungian Analyst and member of the Chicago Society of Jungian Analysts and Interregional Society of Jungian Analysts. She is a faculty member of the C.G. Jung Institute of Chicago and has designed and co-directed the Clinical Training is a senior analyst who has lectured both nationally and internationally on the relationship of Jungian psychology to culture, mythology and religion. She has a full time analytical practice in Chicago.

Fred R. Gustafson, D. Min. is a Diplomate Jungian Analyst (Zurich) and member of the Chicago Society of Jungian Analysts. He is a senior training analyst with the C.G. Jung Institute of Chicago and a clergy member of the Evangelical Lutheran Church in America. He has lectured both nationally and internationally on subjects related to Analytical Psychology and religion. He is the author of *The Black Madonna of Einsiedeln: An Ancient Image for Our Present Time, Dancing Between Two Worlds: Jung and the Native American Soul* and *The Moonlit Path: Reflections on the Dark Feminine.*

You might also enjoy reading these fine Jungian publications

Re-Imagining Mary: A Journey Through Art to the Feminine Self
by Mariann Burke — ISBN 978-0-9810344-1-6

Threshold Experiences: The Archetype of Beginnings
by Michael Conforti— ISBN 978-0-944187-99-9

Marked By Fire: Stories of the Jungian Way
edited by Patricia Damery & Naomi Ruth Lowinsky
— ISBN 978-1-926715-68-1

Farming Soul: A Tale of Initiation
by Patricia Damery — ISBN 978-1-926715-01-8

Transforming Body and Soul:
Therapeutic Wisdom in the Gospel Healing Stories
by Steven Galipeau — ISBN 978-1-926715-62-9

Lifting the Veil
by Fred Gustafson & Jane Kamerling
— ISBN 978-1-926715-75-9

Resurrecting the Unicorn: Masculinity in the 21ˢᵗ Century
by Bud Harris — ISBN 978-0-9810344-0-9

The Father Quest: Rediscovering an Elemental Force
by Bud Harris — ISBN 978-0-9810344-9-2

Like Gold Through Fire: The Transforming Power of Suffering
by Massimilla & Bud Harris — ISBN 978-0-9810344-5-4

The Art of Love: The Craft of Relationship
by Massimilla and Bud Harris — ISBN 978-1-926715-02-5

Divine Madness: Archetypes of Romantic Love
by John R. Haule — ISBN 978-1-926715-04-9

Eros and the Shattering Gaze: Transcending Narcissism
by Ken Kimmel — ISBN 978-1-926715-49-0

The Sister From Below: When the Muse Gets Her Way
by Naomi Ruth Lowinsky — ISBN 978-0-9810344-2-3

The Motherline: Every Woman's Journey to find her Female Roots
by Naomi Ruth Lowinsky — ISBN 978-0-9810344-6-1

The Dairy Farmer's Guide to the Universe: Jung and Ecopsychology
by Dennis Merritt
Volume 1 — ISBN 978-1-926715-42-1
Volume 2 — ISBN 978-1-926715-43-8
Volume 3 — ISBN 978-1-926715-44-5
Volume 4 — ISBN 978-1-926715-45-2

Becoming: An Introduction to Jung's Concept of Individuation
by Deldon Anne McNeely — ISBN 978-1-926715-12-4

Animus Aeternus: Exploring the Inner Masculine
by Deldon Anne McNeely — ISBN 978-1-926715-37-7

Mercury Rising: Women, Evil, and the Trickster Gods
by Deldon Anne McNeely — ISBN 978-1-926715-54-4

Four Eternal Women: Toni Wolff Revisited—A Study In Opposites
by Mary Dian Molton & Lucy Anne Sikes — ISBN 978-1-926715-31-5

Gathering the Light: A Jungian View of Meditation
by V. Walter Odajnyk — ISBN 978-1-926715-55-1

The Promiscuity Papers
by Matjaz Regovec — ISBN 978-1-926715-38-4

Enemy, Cripple, Beggar: Shadows in the Hero's Path
by Erel Shalit — ISBN 978-0-9776076-7-9

The Cycle of Life: Themes and Tales of the Journey
by Erel Shalit — ISBN 978-1-926715-50-6

The Hero and His Shadow:
Psychopolitical Aspects of Myth and Reality in Israel
by Erel Shalit — ISBN 978-1-926715-69-8

The Guilt Cure
by Nancy Carter Pennington & Lawrence H. Staples
— ISBN 978-1-926715-53-7

Guilt with a Twist: The Promethean Way
by Lawrence H. Staples — ISBN 978-0-9776076-4-8

The Creative Soul: Art and the Quest for Wholeness
by Lawrence H. Staples — ISBN 978-0-9810344-4-7

Deep Blues: Human Soundscapes for the Archetypal Journey
by Mark Winborn — ISBN 978-1-926715-52-0

Fisher King Press publishes an eclectic mix of worthy books including
Jungian Psychological Perspectives, Cutting-Edge Fiction, Poetry, and a
growing list of Alternative titles.

Phone Orders Welcomed — Credit Cards Accepted
In Canada & the U.S. call 1-800-228-9316
International call +1-831-238-7799
www.fisherkingpress.com

Made in the USA
San Bernardino, CA
18 January 2018